Praise for *The Stargazer*

"Once in a great while, an author captures your heart and head with poignant lessons about life and leadership. Michael and Katie have scored twice! In their new book *The Stargazer*, the reader travels through the magic and wonders of the universe while exploring life lessons and reflections on the implications of how vast our potential is for interconnectedness. For educators, the implications for transfer to instructional leadership are significant. A must read for all who wander and wonder."

—Kari Montgomery,
Executive Director of Teaching and Learning

"A captivating read that inspires and serves as a guiding hand for leaders on their journey toward success. Through compelling anecdotes and 'Be mindsets,' *The Stargazer* encourages readers to reframe their thinking while identifying both areas of strength and areas of potential growth. Most of all, *The Stargazer* provides leaders with an understanding of how to build their own 'star systems' and lead with a strong network and support system surrounding them. *The Stargazer* is a must-read for anyone looking to sharpen their leadership skills and build brilliant, shining star teams. "

—Liz Elting,
Wall Street Journal *Bestselling Author, CEO,*
and Philanthropist

"*The Stargazer* is a beacon for leaders aspiring to cultivate radiant, high-performing teams. It offers invaluable insights into harnessing the collective brilliance of individuals to achieve extraordinary results. Most importantly, it reminds us that as leaders we must always focus on storytelling and encouraging our teams to also share in these stories because ultimately it is always about the power of We."

—Geoffrey M. Roche,
North America Director, Workforce Development,
Siemens Healthineers

"*The Stargazer* weaves together everything we know about leadership and team development: self-reflection, learning, curiosity, clarity, shared purpose, and more. Nuggets of wisdom and learning are as brilliant and plentiful as the stars themselves."

—Marci Lesko,
CEO, United Way

"Enticing, informing, and motivating. . .educational but also heartwarming. Introspection, understanding one's own motivations translated into purpose comes alive with a main character who is easy to identify with quickly. *The Stargazer* translates well known effective principles into digestible and memorable models that help everyone become more effective in his or her professional and personal lives. Enjoy!"

—**Dr. Allen Weiss,**
Chief Medical Officer, Blue Zones Project

"*The Stargazer* brilliantly illuminates the path to building brighter, more resilient teams. Through its captivating fable, the book demonstrates how leaders can cultivate an environment of growth, collaboration, and shared purpose. It's a must-read for anyone committed to unleashing the full potential of their team and leading with intentionality and heart."

—**Tony Martignetti,**
Chief Inspiration Officer, Inspired Purpose Partners,
and Author of
Campfire Lessons for Leaders

"*The Stargazer* is a quick but powerful read that will make you stop, reflect, and think. Katie and Michael pull you into a story filled with valuable lessons and insights to help you unite your team. This book is a must-read if you aspire to be a better leader or more supportive teammate."

—**Aaron Burton,**
CEO, Sciton

"Incorporating stargazing and outdoor experiential learning is brilliant. It's amazing what we can learn about ourselves and others when we disconnect in the outdoors and put ourselves in the present moment, but even more amazing how it positively impacts our personal and professional lives. The COMPASS framework is brilliant and a tool all leaders can leverage to navigate their teams up the trail to their summit of growth and development."

—Dan Carusi,
President, Red Paint Consulting

"There is brilliance in these pages. Desiderio's and Frino's message is profound: As individuals, the lens we choose determines what we see. When we choose to demonstrate care, competence, consistency, and commitment to ourselves and those around us, we build a star system that enables each individual to shine brighter. With the proper mindset, we can achieve personal and organizational growth."

—David Robinson,
EVP, Human Resources and General Counsel, ArtSkills Inc.

"The beauty of nature and the universe holds deep meaning in our lives. In this compelling fable, Katie and Michael gently reveal valuable lessons for every leader. As they guide us on a journey of reconnection with timeless truths, they help us align not only ourselves but also our teams and organizations, like stars in a brilliant constellation. This book is a warm and inspiring guide, lighting the way to more thoughtful, impactful leadership."

—Ximena Duran,
Business Relationship Manager, Grupo GOCA

"Stargazer is not just a beautiful story about the importance of self-discovery; it is about how we can help others shine, appreciate those who help us too, and understand ourselves as a community that can grow and create. It is about building something much bigger by seeing ourselves as a team. Thank you for this fable that teaches us to learn and unlearn. By looking through the stars, we discover how great and bright we can be, and understand the value of the elements that always enrich and nurture us."

—Luis Fernando,
Director of Strategy, Grupo GOCA

"Stargazer could simply be an engaging read. Or, more likely, it subtly layers lesson after lesson for the reader, where the reader can choose to reconsider what it means to grow, to change, to succeed with and through others, and perhaps most importantly, what it means to experience a personal transformation."

—Dr. Bill Schaninger,
Partner, Modern Executive Solutions;
Speaker and Author

"The Stargazer is an inspiring leadership fable that beautifully intertwines the wonders of the night sky with the journey of personal and professional growth. Grayce's transformation, guided by her mentor Catherine, is a testament to the power of choosing your lens each day and the importance of having a supportive 'star system' in one's life. The narrative is both engaging and thought-provoking, offering practical lessons on how to cultivate curiosity, resilience, and connectedness. This book is a must-read for anyone looking to ignite their inner brilliance and lead with empathy and innovation."

—Thomas C Murray,
Director of Innovation, Future Ready Schools,
ASCD Bestselling Author

"In *The Stargazer*, Katie Desiderio and Michael Frino, the bestselling authors of *The Beekeeper*, once again craft a compelling fable that delves into the dynamics of high-functioning teams and the critical roles of key individuals in driving success. Written in a style reminiscent of Patrick Lencioni, Desiderio and Frino narrate the powerful story of Jack, who embarks on a quest for meaning in both his personal life and business endeavors. Through Jack's journey, the authors illustrate how the insights he gains can be applied to corporate team-building retreats. This book is essential reading for any CEO aiming to cultivate a high-performing team."

—Dr. Bryon Grigsby,
President and Professor of English, Moravian College

"*The Stargazer* masterfully weaves celestial metaphors to illustrate the transformative power of curiosity and learning. Readers will soon find themselves inspired or 'star-kissed,' embracing their 'star system' of friends, colleagues, and mentors as they critically reflect on their own experiences to better navigate life's challenges and uncover profound meaning in every opportunity that comes their way."

—Dr. David Kopp,
Author, Speaker CAMPUS.EDU

"Grayce, a character from the bestselling *The Beekeeper*, has become a pollinator. She is successfully spreading growth and enlightenment; she is being proximal. Inspired by the 'Be mindsets,' this new fable from Katie and Mike details the leadership journey of a small business owner. Jack learns to embrace the lessons from the stars and the stones to dramatically alter the trajectory of his small winery.

An engaging story set in the vineyards and rugged terrain of northern California, this is a natural continuation of the shared leadership lessons that can be learned and adopted by anyone."

—Dr. Larry Ross,
Professor Emeritus, Barnett School of Business, Florida Southern College

"Desiderio and Frino have done it again. Set this time on a corporate retreat, the story expertly exposes us to the secrets of building brilliance through harnessing collective strength. A must-read for all executives and managers who tend to their organization's morale and efficacy. If you liked *The Beekeeper*, you will love *The Stargazer!*"

—Michele Demsky,
President and CEO, ArtSkills Inc.

"The use of narrative and fable makes *Stargazer's* lessons accessible to a variety of audiences, from high school and college students to practicing business professionals. In its humanity—its encouragement to pursue learning and meaning through the mutual support required to achieve group goals—it strikes an implicit blow against the shareholder capitalism and profit maximization that has deformed our economy and society more generally."

—Galen Godbey,
Professor and Author

"Yet again, Katie Desiderio and Michael Frino thread the needle for the perfect blend of storytelling and management science for an engaging read. *The Stargazer's* principles through story show a unique perspective on how to magnify your impact on your team and organization. This book allows you to read at your own pace, reflecting after each chapter to journal your key 'Be Brilliant' learnings. The authors show how Jack used what he learned with the COMPASS approach to apply these principles in a leadership retreat. This book would make for a great journal club with leaders in any organization."

—Brian McGee,
Director of Sales, Boston Scientific

"An enjoyable, educational, and thought-provoking story, with constant opportunities for reflection to benefit all aspects of our lives, not just for leaders but anyone who wants to be proximal. Be present, be vulnerable as you take in this motivating tale of personal reflection. May we all see challenges as opportunities for growth."

—Karyn McClintick,
School Counselor, Central Dauphin Middle School

"Desiderio and Frino did it again! *The Stargazer* is a thought-provoking read that can be used to encourage teams to embrace curiosity, build meaningful relationships, and strive for their own personal growth. It's a reminder that, like stars in the sky, we all have the ability to shine brightly when we step out of our comfort zone and reach out to connect with others. I highly recommend this book to anyone looking to embrace their sense of wonder, explore their purpose, or inspire those around them to do the same. I am so excited to use their newest fable to inspire our team!"

—Tara Desiderio,
Public School Principal

"*The Stargazer* captures its readers with charming characters that share profound leadership lessons in a relatable way. The story is compact but the lessons are vast. A must-read for all C-suite executives who care about organizational culture and staff development. I can't wait to share this with my teams and watch the individual and collective learnings unfold."

—Dr. Nicole Loyd,
EVP, COO and Dean of Students, Moravian University

"Katie and Mike have done it again! Another *powerful* book that outlines the practical steps to take teams to new heights!"

—Jon Alwinson,
Sales Leader and Author of Relentless Sales

"Being pollinated directly with *The Beekeeper* pushed the limits of my growth mindset. Now *The Stargazer* has aligned my COMPASS towards shining brighter with my own star network! May we all continue to be brilliant. Thank you, Katie and Michael!"

—Dr. Dawn Sparks,
Physician/Owner/Founder/Medical Director

"*The Stargazer* is a must-read for any team wanting a transformative experience. The reflections in the story are ones that have the potential to take your team from ordinary to brilliant. The messages are meaningful, thought-provoking, and profound. After reading this book, you will feel compelled to create your very own star system: a system of people who light up your life, help you illuminate things you may not see, and create a picture of what is and what could be."

—Dr. Monica Law,
Professor of Management

"*The Stargazer* is an inspiring story, and a must-read for any leader who wants to captivate their team while taking them to the next level of productivity. As a CEO and founder of an employee benefits company I encourage everyone to read this book; there is not one person who would not relate and be inspired. Katie and Michael have outdone themselves."

—Tony DaRe,
CEO, BSI Corporate Benefits

"Another masterpiece by Katie Desiderio and Michael Frino, *The Stargazer* uses the power of storytelling to inspire readers to embark on their own journeys of personal growth. Katie and Mike's work has not only inspired readers like myself to reevaluate my focus and approach as a leader but has also provided practical strategies to leverage the strengths and abilities of the teams I lead. *The Stargazer* is more than just a book—it is a guide for anyone looking to transform their leadership practices, foster team collaboration, and build a brighter future."

—Melanie Fike,
Senior Director, Professional Learning and Instructional Resources

A LEADERSHIP FABLE

THE

Stargazer

UNLEASHING THE BRILLIANCE OF BUILDING BRIGHTER TEAMS

Katie P. Desiderio *and* Michael G. Frino
Bestselling Authors of *The Beekeeper*

WILEY

Library of Congress Cataloging-in-Publication Data

Names: Desiderio, Katie P. author | Frino, Michael G. author | John Wiley & Sons publisher
Title: The stargazer : unleashing the brilliance of building brighter teams / Katie Desiderio, Michael Frino.
Description: Hoboken, New Jersey : Wiley, [2025] | Includes bibliographical references and index.
Identifiers: LCCN 2024038140 (print) | LCCN 2024038141 (ebook) | ISBN 9781394280537 hardback | ISBN 9781394280544 epub | ISBN 9781394280551 adobe pdf
Subjects: LCSH: Career development | Employees--Training of | Personnel management
Classification: LCC HF5549.5.C35 D465 2025 (print) | LCC HF5549.5.C35 (ebook) | DDC 658.3/124--dc23/eng/20240930
LC record available at https://lccn.loc.gov/2024038140
LC ebook record available at https://lccn.loc.gov/2024038141

Cover art & design: Paul McCarthy
SKY10098759_022025

Contents

Preface   *xv*

Prologue: Starkissed   *xvii*

Chapter 1   *Star*struck   1

Chapter 2   First *Star*   5

Chapter 3   *Star*link   15

Chapter 4   *Star*burst   23

Chapter 5   *Star*light   35

Chapter 6   Co*star*   49

Chapter 7   Super*star*   59

Chapter 8   Be*star*red   65

Chapter 9   *Star*gaze   75

Chapter 10   Proto*star*   89

Chapter 11   Lode*star*   99

Chapter 12   Rockstar   111

Chapter 13   Starbright   119

Chapter 14   Stars and Stones   131

A Leadership Guide to Unleashing the
Brilliance of Building Brighter Teams   141
Acknowledgments   173
About the Authors   175
Index   179

Preface

When our first book, *The Beekeeper: Pollinating Your Organization for Transformative Growth*, became a *Wall Street Journal* Business Bestseller in 2023, we were amazed by its impact on people, teams, and organizations.

As first-time authors, the energy from our star system fueled the creation of this second book. From scribbled chapter names on a dinner menu to research at wolf sanctuaries, on trails, and with astronomers, a fable emerged about unleashing the brilliance of building brighter teams.

During a spring equinox visit to our publisher, we reviewed a contract for two more leadership fables. Fast forward, one year later, we celebrate this day of happiness with the launch of *The Stargazer: Unleashing the Brilliance of Building Brighter Teams*. Will you join us in shining brighter, together?

Prologue

Starkissed

Grayce had always been a stargazer, but only recently had she truly felt starkissed. Ever since she met her friend Catherine, her life was different. It was Catherine who had nurtured Grayce and helped her learn to be proximal – to place herself at the center of her own growth and that of the people around her. She taught Grayce how "Be mindsets" could change the way she looked at the world and also provide a roadmap for areas of personal growth.

Grayce knew she'd always had a tendency to be curious, but she hadn't been enacting this as an actual mindset. Catherine helped Grayce understand what it meant to identify the mindsets that were her greatest strengths and also explore the mindsets that didn't come naturally, where she might need a growth partner or someone to support her.

Grayce found such a growth partner in Catherine, who had a passion for beehives and how the lessons of pollinators could help people become more fulfilled in their lives. Catherine inspired Grayce to get out of her comfort zone and become a "Be Keeper" and really demonstrate what it meant to place herself at the core of learning and growth, or in other words, how to Be Proximal. Grayce took this seriously and decided to own her Be mindsets and went on a journey to pollinate others, just as Catherine had pollinated her. Grayce wanted to share this message with others and show up with the Be mindsets that could help them grow. At the core she would have the Be mindset to Be Proximal, but her other strengths were to Be Curious, Be Bright, Be Reflective, and Be Connected.

A network of people helped her determine how she could be a pollinator. Her network included Catherine, who she felt was a growth partner for her; her father, who was always a source of wisdom; and her principal at the school where she'd worked for eight years. She also had her best friend, Karyn, who knew every last detail about her since they were kids, and her older sister, who could not be more supportive and encouraging. She called these five people in her life her star system. This group of individuals lit up her life, helped illuminate things she might not see, and created a picture of what was and what could be. Without Grayce's star system, she would not have experienced the fulfillment and happiness she felt today. Thanks to her star system, Grayce felt truly blessed and starkissed. Her focus would now be to place herself at the core of learning and growth both for herself and for others – in her full-time job as a teacher, her volunteer work at the state park, and her daily experiences with everyone she met.

CHAPTER 1

*Star*struck

"Are you Jack from Stars and Stones?" someone asked me while I was sitting on the train.

I looked up and smiled, and soon we were having a conversation. It felt surreal to have someone you've never met recognize you on a train and call you by name.

Only 18 months earlier, I'd wondered if my small wine-making business would thrive. The vineyard I had purchased was fledgling and had no identity. It seemed to be much more of a project than I had originally hoped for.

Everything changed with my trip to a local state park, where I met my new friend Grayce, who helped me to embrace a growth mindset. I was starstruck by her approach to life. Thanks to Grayce, I learned to recognize what was happening in my life, reflect on what was and could be, and connect with others more personally. It was a real catalyst for change in my life.

Ever since my trip to the park, I'd had a clear vision of what impact I wanted to have in this world, who could help me, and a renewed spirit to create transformative growth. I knew that if I prioritized the human element rather than the mundane tasks of running a business, it would be truly transformative.

Now my inventory was flying off the shelves, people were calling to come visit our vineyard, and my social media followers were in the hundreds of thousands. My videos, which had previously been outside my comfort zone, were going viral. My content was inspiring people, and the comments and messages I'd received had been heartwarming and humbling. Strangers were even striking up conversations with me on trains. Maybe just as I'd been starstruck by my friend Grayce, I might be reaching and helping others, and as they carried the same lessons forward, others would be starstruck by them.

Thinking about this sent me down a nostalgic path to the day when I had met Grayce, just 18 months earlier. . . .

CHAPTER
2

First *Star*

Camping was not a go-to activity for me, but it was something my close group of friends resolved we would all do together in early June. Although our trips traditionally had been for golfing or attending a sporting event, this time we decided to hit up my local state park and do a few hikes. The plan was to meet my friends at the park and go to the campground to spend Tuesday through Saturday together.

The campground was a five-hour drive for me, but my friends Tye and Antonio were flying together from Florida, which was about an eight-hour flight on Tuesday morning and then a one-hour drive. So they had a much larger commitment to this trip. I was a little bit excited because I had not seen these friends since I moved to Yountville, California, and I wanted to make sure everything would be all set when they arrived. I decided to go to the campsite a day early, on Monday, to get the lay of the land. I'd read some great online reviews of the park and trail, but I wanted to check out the area for myself and verify information about the trails with some park staff.

The park had entrances on the north, south, east, and west sides. Next to the "Welcome to Kaleidoscope Moon Park, East entrance" wooden sign, a park ranger collected money for parking. I rolled down the window, paid my $25, and was handed a pass for the week with some rules and hours of operation. Customer service might not have been part of the training, but nevertheless he gave a nod when I said a jovial goodbye.

According to the information I received, the snow had melted since it was June, but this raises a potential concern, as mudslides could lead to unstable hiking conditions. The pamphlet also said the park's visitors center was closing in about two hours, and I wanted to learn more about the park and the hikes we could go on. The drive there was amazing – mountains toward the south side of the park, as well as plenty of open spaces for viewing wildlife. Near the visitors center in the middle of the park, I pulled my white truck in one of the gravel parking spaces delineated with logs to help guests identify where to stop. I got out of the truck and stretched. I could see a few deer grazing in the grass nearby, minding their own business as guests walked about. I made my way into the visitors center, walking stiffly like someone who had been in a vehicle for five hours. My back was a bit tight and I knew I would need to do some serious stretching to loosen up my muscles before I hit the trails.

The visitors center was just as one might imagine: a desk, a corkboard with pictures of wildlife that had been spotted, a rack with postcards, maps, brochures, and some souvenirs. There was a cooler with drinks and a freezer with standard ice pops and ice cream bars. A large poster of the park at night with a star-filled sky caught my eye. It was mesmerizing, like some of those surreal pictures from the Hubble or Webb telescope I'd seen on the Internet. A voice interrupted my thoughts.

"Good evening. What can I help you with?" A smiling woman emerged from a back room behind the desk. She was dressed in a park ranger outfit of khaki pants and a fitted white shirt with some patches and a "Welcome to the Park" button. Her crisp cap sported the park logo, and her nametag said Isabella.

"Hi, Isabella. I'm Jack. It's nice to meet you. I'm doing a group trip with some friends. We've got a number of things planned, but I wanted to get some information on the park and what hikes and activities you'd recommend for us," I said.

"That sounds fun! How long will you be here?"

"Until Saturday," I answered.

"Well, you'll have a great time at the park. There's so much to do, and the time will just fly by."

She inquired about our fitness level and stamina, and about the overall experience we hoped for. I explained that we wanted to do increasingly difficult hikes that challenged us but also provided amazing views.

She opened up a laminated map with all the trails and hikes we could explore. She also helped me download the park app, which included GPS, so we could navigate the trails and not get lost. She starred her favorite trails that she thought we should do. Some of these were already on our list, but some were a little off the beaten path and required a drive to get there. She reviewed some of the other available activities, too. There were swimming holes, natural springs, a sporting clay range, and other evening events, such as stargazing.

My discussion with Isabella was interrupted by a ping notifying me about a text from Tye on my group text chain: *Delayed.*

"Excuse me for a minute," I said. Isabella nodded.

I stepped away, called my buddy Tye, and asked what was going on. He said their flight was delayed about four hours, so they likely wouldn't get in until early Tuesday evening unless things changed. I told him not to worry and to keep me posted, and we got off the phone.

"Everything alright?" Isabella asked.

"Just a delay with my friends, but everything is okay. Thanks for asking," I said.

Isabella and I wrapped up our conversation, and she handed me the laminated map and an activity brochure. She encouraged me to grab some BBQ at the main park lodge before heading out to the campground a few miles deeper into the park.

I was hungry so I took her up on the suggestion and headed over to the park lodge. There were long community tables, but I tend to be a little introverted and didn't feel like mingling, so I found a separate picnic table and placed my informational brochures and maps on the table to reserve my seat. I walked over to the BBQ line to check it out. They had chicken, ribs, pulled pork, hamburgers, and hot dogs, along with a salad bar and plenty of vegetables. I loaded my plate up with some veggies and made myself a pulled pork sandwich. Even though the baked beans looked amazing, I decided to pass on them for reasons that might seem obvious to anyone on a five-day hiking trip. I made sure to grab a water, because staying hydrated was going to be key for a week of challenging hikes. I returned to my previously empty table, where a woman was now sitting. As I approached, I gave myself a pep talk to be cordial.

"Hi! I'm Grayce," she called out cheerfully.

"I'm Jack. Nice to meet you," I replied.

"I hope you don't mind me sitting here. So many of the tables were full, and I figured you might want some company." She smiled.

Grayce must have been in her early 30s, with chin-length hair, hazel eyes, and toned arms. She wore a tank top, and a ballcap with the image of a mountain. Her plate was full of vegetables and a piece of BBQ chicken.

"What brings you here?" she asked.

"My friends and I are doing a group trip this week and we wanted to visit state park and do some hiking and exploring."

"That sounds wonderful! Hiking is so much fun, and you've come to the right place to do it!" Grayce said.

"So you hike here often?" I asked.

"Oh, I work here in the evenings. I'm an earth-space science high school teacher by day, and I come to the park at night and set up my telescopes. I have a passion for astronomy and love astrology, so it's how I can Be Nourished after work. I'm an amateur astronomer, which means I know enough to be dangerous," she grinned.

"That's interesting. I was looking at a nice picture of the night sky in the visitors center. The stars aren't something I've ever really had the opportunity to learn about and explore, but they're fascinating and mysterious."

"Well, you'll have to come over in a little while and let me show them to you. The best time is around 8 or 9 p.m., just after sunset." Grayce said. "This park has some of the best sky for observing the stars. There isn't much light pollution here, so you can really see clearly."

Although the offer was tempting, I wasn't sure I had the energy for it. "It's been a long day of travel, and. . ."

Before I could object, Grayce said, "Oh, now don't back out on me. You said you're interested in the stars. Be curious on your vacation. Call your friends and have them swing by, too."

"Oh, my friends come in tomorrow, so it's just me tonight."

"So there's no reason not to come take a peek," she said, winking.

"So how did you get into astronomy?"

Her face lit up. I could sense she was about to talk my ear off, and I realized my question might have been a little too open-ended.

She told me about growing up in California, loving science, always wanting to be a science teacher, and getting her master's in education and a minor in astronomy. She loved the night sky, and when she was a kid she had a poster of Van Gogh's *Starry Night* on her wall, and glow-in-the-dark stars stuck to her ceiling.

I must admit I had those, too – they were kind of cool. I remember coming home from college after seven years and they were still there. My parents asked me to remove them, and some ceiling paint ripped off with each one. That prompted them to tell me to repaint the ceiling, which had a textured finish. So basically it would have been better to just keep the stars up there because now there was ceiling with a bunch of crummy touch-up paint instead of a glowing solar system. The conversation with Grayce had made me a bit nostalgic, and I suddenly realized my internal reflection had made me miss a bunch of what she was saying.

I quickly became more present, nodded, and engaged a little more meaningfully with her. I had been eating the whole time and noticed she barely took a bite of her food, so I found the perfect spot to interject.

"Grayce," I said, "this is fascinating, but you haven't taken a bite. Why don't you take a minute to eat?"

In my attempt to be kind and respectful, I'd given Grayce a window to ask me an open-ended question of her own.

"So tell me about you, Jack." Sensing my hesitation to open up, she quickly added, "Hey, look at all those people gathering by my telescopes."

Nearby, four telescopes pointed in four different directions like a compass. The telescopes sat in a huge circle of rope that was big enough to hold four adults and maybe Grayce to do some teaching. Kids and adults were gathering around outside the circle. The sign said, "Come meet the Stargazer. Discussion and viewing begins at 8:30, right around sunset."

"It looks like you're getting quite the following already," I said. "Why are they all at that circle?"

She smiled, "So you're curious! That circle represents a compass and helps point to different directions in the sky, but more importantly it's also the core of learning and growth for everyone who steps inside."

"The core of learning and growth," I repeated.

"That's right! You see, to be centered or at the heart of something means to Be Proximal. Proximal means closest to the heart. When people come here to stargaze, they're demonstrating a learner's mind. They are curious, present, and vulnerable. You said it earlier, Jack. The sky is mysterious and fascinating. Sometimes we don't appreciate nature's beauty and all the lessons it has to teach us."

She backed away from the table and picked up her plate. She thanked me for the company and reminded me to pop over and check out the stars.

"The best time to gaze is around 9 o'clock. Come by in a couple hours and take a peek," she said.

I smiled and nodded and said I would stop by, and off Grayce went. She stood right in the middle of that rope circle and people gathered around. I watched as she pointed to the sky. It was only 7:30 p.m., so I figured I would check into my cabin and freshen up, hopefully not fall asleep, and go peek at the stars around 9:00 p.m.

I jumped in my truck. As I backed away and the dust kicked up from the gravel road, I could see more people walking over to the telescopes. It seemed like there was a lot of interest in the stars. I could see the first early star appear just above the horizon as I drove up the road.

CHAPTER
3

*Star*link

When I got to the campsite I tried to navigate and find our cabin. There weren't many lights outside to guide you, which I assumed was to reduce the light pollution. I was grateful for that because the stars did seem brighter. I finally found the cabin, grabbed my luggage and cooler from the truck, and unlocked the door. It was a two-bedroom suite with a small living area and kitchen. The place smelled a bit like cedar or pine, which I guess added to the experience. I figured my friends wouldn't mind if I took the room with the view. I laid on the bed, grabbed my phone, and touched base with Tye and Antonio. Their flight was still departing late. I was so exhausted from the day and just wanted to lie there and decompress. However, I'd told Grayce I would pop over and look through her telescopes. I set an alarm for 8:45, closed my eyes, and reflected.

When I was growing up, my parents had encouraged me to help my uncle Mike on his small vineyard in Yountville, California. As an adult, I'd continued helping him during my summer break from teaching. After retiring early at the age of 47, I needed a new challenge. When I had the opportunity to partner with Uncle Mike on his vineyard, I jumped at the chance. Sadly, my aunt fell ill one year after I partnered with him. Uncle Mike had been there for me when I had lost my parents, and I wanted to be there for him. With my aunt gone, he didn't have the heart to continue running the vineyard and wanted to sell it. After a lifetime of helping him, I had some understanding of the business, and I thought buying him out would be a great thing. But I had no idea about the difficulties and stress I would encounter in the coming year. It turned out to be a real challenge, and I was hemorrhaging my savings to keep the vineyard afloat. Despite what I'd learned from my uncle, the learning curve for making and marketing wine was still very steep.

When my alarm went off, I let out a huge sigh. I got up from the comfortable bed, brushed my teeth, and decided to make my way to the telescope. I hopped in my truck and began to drive to the visitors center. Along the way, I spotted a sign saying to watch for children and to keep only parking lights on. I adjusted the lights and slowed my speed. When I parked, I could see Grayce talking to an older couple. It was quieter than when the BBQ was going on, despite this being the best time to look at the stars. The night was a bit cloudy so I was curious if we would see anything. Either way, being out in nature was truly inspiring and gave me a sense of purpose.

Grayce spotted me and waved me over. She was just finishing her conversation with the couple, and they thanked her for their time.

"Hello, Jack," she said.

I gave a nod and said hello back.

"How has the stargazing been?" I asked.

"The traffic has been nonstop," Grayce said.

"Have you seen anything interesting?" I glanced skyward and could make out a thin crescent moon and a few bright stars between the sporadic clouds.

"Well, it's been a bit cloudy tonight, but there are some things you can see. The people stopping by ask so many great questions, and the kids all have a thirst for understanding the universe. Come into the circle, and I'll point out a couple things." Grayce motioned me inside. "You recall what the circle is called?" she asked.

"The center of growth, I think."

"Close. It's the core of learning and growth. Come look through this telescope." She pointed to the telescope facing west.

The clouds were currently parting, so there was a window of opportunity for us. I peered through the eyepiece but couldn't really see anything. Noticing that I was struggling, Grayce peered through it and made a minor adjustment. She pointed to the sky and explained that I should be looking at the big bright spot next to the moon. I peered through and saw what appeared to be a circular planet. I backed away quickly.

"Is it a planet?" I inquired.

"Yes, it is. June is the perfect month to spot Venus and Mars in the night sky. Mars is that distant dot, but Venus shines so bright," she said full of energy.

"Do you know anything about Venus, Jack?"

"Just that she's the goddess of love, it's a neighboring planet to Earth, and they make razor blades for women" I joked.

Grayce chuckled and then explained, "Venus is about love and harmony with our emotional attachments, in life, friendships, and other unions, like business partnerships that help us to be brilliant. It's said that the planet Venus spreads joy and happiness while teaching us how to love and appreciate others. Because of Venus's good energy, socializing and relating to others is very important to this planet."

As Grayce was talking, I was peering again at the planet through the telescope. It was more beautiful now that I had gained some insight. I raised my head from the telescope and looked at Grayce.

"That was so interesting," I told her. She nodded.

"You know, Jack, it's not just relationships that Venus is associated with. The planet is inextricably linked to culture and the finer things in life such as good food and wine."

"Wine?" I said.

"Yes! Good food and wine. The planet asks us to appreciate the beauty of the world and the nature of things. Like a fine wine."

"Wait. Did I tell you that I own a winery?"

"No! Isn't it funny how the universe works, Jack? That is the power of Venus. Aside from the moon, she's the brightest object in the sky right now."

I peered again but could no longer see Venus. Grayce made an adjustment to the telescope, and I checked it again.

"Why does it look so fuzzy through the telescope?" I asked.

"Venus has a permanent cloud cover, so its true brilliance lies beneath the clouds," she said.

I looked up at her and nodded.

"Sometimes brilliance is clouded, but the right lens can help us to see, Jack. On that note, I need to close shop because I teach tomorrow morning and need to go home and get some rest. But I hope to hear more about your winery! Maybe you'll swing by tomorrow with your friends."

"Sure thing. How often do you come here?" I asked.

"Monday through Friday from 7:30 to 9:30. It fuels me," she said as she started breaking down the telescopes.

I offered to help in packing up, but she declined. "Don't let the clouds covering Venus distract you from its true beauty and importance. The importance of finding emotionally strong relationships, an appreciation of the finer things in life, and the link to nature is what makes Venus so special. What we see, Jack, depends mainly on what lens we choose."

I thanked Grayce and made my way back to my cabin. I opened a small journal that had been a gift from a friend. I kept my thoughts and ideas in the journal, which was about halfway complete. I moved the journal's ribbon page holder and started a new page. I titled the page "Be Brilliant" and wrote down some reflections that I could not stop thinking about from my conversations with Grayce.

Be Brilliant

Monday 10:00 p.m.

To be centered or at the heart of something means to Be Proximal, which means closest to the heart. When people come to Kaleidoscope Moon Park to stargaze, they are demonstrating a learner's mind. How can I be curious, present, and vulnerable? How can I appreciate nature's beauty and all the lessons?

What we see depends mainly on what lens we choose. I am still processing what this means. I am not sure I pay attention to what I see beyond surface level. Is this what it means to choose my lens?

Venus is linked to harmony, nature, culture, and the finer things in life — much like wine. This one makes a lot of sense to me. I am sending a shout-up to heaven to you, Mom. You always reminded me that the universe is powerful. I can feel you with me in spirit.

What were your Be Brilliant key learnings?

_____

_____

_____

_____

_____

_____

_____

CHAPTER 4

Starburst

On Tuesday morning, I woke up early. I'd had a restless night. I couldn't stop thinking about my conversation with Grayce and the vineyard, and I was looking forward to seeing my friends. I decided to do a hike on my own to get the blood flowing. I'd always valued working out because it was a great way to start the day and helped me achieve balance in my life. While it wasn't always easy to find the time, I tried to prioritize it.

I pulled open the laminated map of all the hikes Isabella had given me at the visitors center. I then quickly pivoted online to look at some of the reviews, images, and difficulty levels. I wanted to choose a moderately challenging hike that would be rigorous but enjoyable at the same time. Also, I didn't want to be exhausted and sore when my friends arrived, because I knew they'd want to hit the trails.

There were so many hikes to choose from, all with different variations, scenery, and elevations. I had already identified some hikes for our group, but looking at the more moderate hikes to try alone today felt a little daunting. In the end, I used trail names to plan a two-hour hike that really looked inspiring.

Just then my phone rang. It was Antonio.

"Hey, are you heading to the airport?" I asked.

"We were planning on it, but the departing flight got pushed another hour, and we're going to miss our connection in Dallas, so we're trying to figure out a plan."

"That's awful. Anything I can do to help?"

"No, just stay tuned. Hopefully we can find something, and the airline can help us out. We may look at another airline, too."

"Okay. Thanks for letting me know. Talk soon and keep in touch."

"Will do," Antonio said.

Then I texted to the group chat: *Sorry about the flight! Let me know when you have things sorted out.*

There was some commiserating on the group chat, and I could sense some frustration. This could impact the entire trip.

I got dressed and walked to the visitors center from the cabin. It was about a mile, so not a big deal. Some of the trails started there, so I figured my friends and I would make this walk regularly. The hike entrances were near the same spot where I'd been looking at the sky the night before. I grabbed a bite to eat from the continental breakfast buffet near the visitors center, filled up my water bottle, and took an apple and a banana for the road. I opened the trail app on my phone to determine which direction to head. While staring down at the app, I started walking toward the trails and nearly tripped as my foot hit something. Strangely, it was the rope from last night that formed the circle on the ground around the core of learning and growth. I stepped inside and kind of laughed to myself. I would have expected Grayce to pick this up and take it with her.

"Hey, there," a park ranger said.

"Good morning," I replied.

He approached me and asked, "Can I help you find something?"

"I was looking for the trail to Reflection Lake via the valley on the app." I looked at his name tag, which said Vincent. "Do you know where that is, Vincent?"

"I most certainly do. but first, do you know where we are?" he asked.

I looked around, not really understanding the question.

"We're standing exactly in the center of the park. This rope was placed here years ago by the Indigenous people who lived here. Before this place was even a park, this was the best place to look up to the heavens on a starry night."

I looked up at the blue sky and admired it. I could picture the faint image of the crescent moon from last night and agreed with him.

As I looked down at the rope, I could now see its age, the stakes that were driven through the cordage to keep it in place, and its ends burned to prevent fraying. A plaque on the ground that went unnoticed last night gave the coordinates: 37°44′33″N 119°32′15″W.

"Interesting, huh?" Vincent said. "Now let me point you in the right direction." He showed me the road to the trail, and I thanked him and went on my way.

I stopped for a moment at the trailhead, snapped a selfie with the trail sign, and then continued onward.

As I walked along the gravel path, I could see the mountain range form a stark silhouette against a lake. I realized that must be Reflection Lake. The trees were reflected on the water's surface like a landscape painting on a canvas. The path did not head toward the lake, but I felt compelled to stray from the path to take a closer look. The open field leading to the lake was relatively flat and easy to navigate.

As I got closer, I could sense the insect population getting more excited at my presence. I made my way to the bank of the lake and could see the clear rocky bottom. I squatted down. I could see my reflection as well. Everything was so peaceful and still. I stood up to admire the full beauty of the trees and mountains reflected across the canvas of the lake's surface.

I picked up a stone the size of a golf ball and in a childlike fashion threw it into the water. The ripples from the rock disturbed the canvas, blurring the scene. I could no longer see the mountains, trees, or my own reflection clearly, yet there was such beauty in the disruption. The ripples continued extending outward and the concentric circles kept getting bigger and bigger. The water gradually calmed and the canvas once again showed the mountains, trees, and my image. I could see why this was called Reflection Lake.

As I returned from the lake to the trail and continued my hike, I realized there was deeper symbolism to the lake. Such a small disturbance on the surface can change the way things look and carry the impact with them. I began to think about how this related to the small disturbances in my life that seemed to cause such stress and impact so much. Maybe the ripples they create can have their own beauty, too.

I walked the remaining three miles to complete the loop and snacked on the apple I brought. When I got to the end of the trail loop, there was a large slab of stone with an informational sign that read:

This stone is starburst jasper and is used to improve insight and clarify what your best self looks like. It balances and creates celestial harmony. Starburst jasper may also allow fluidity through the body, removing blockages and increasing the mind and body connection.

This reminded me of something striking that Grayce had said the previous night. What we see depends mainly on what lens we choose! I decided that leaning into disturbances and chaos in life and appreciating them for what they were was the lens I should be choosing. It gave me pause to ask myself if I needed to clarify my purpose so I could be the best version of myself.

I took out my phone and snapped a photo of the large stone and the sign. I returned to my cabin and opened my journal and phone, and wrote down the trail name and the information about starburst jasper right below the insights from the previous night's conversation with Grayce.

A call came in from Antonio. He and Tye couldn't catch a flight and decided to get a refund for their tickets. It looked like this group trip was going to be a bust. I had a choice to make. Did I want to stay and go at it alone over the next few days, or head back home?

I grabbed some lunch in the park restaurant and continued to struggle with my decision. If I left now, I could be home by 8:00 p.m. and go back to work on Wednesday. As I was eating, I saw Vincent, the park ranger, grabbing a cup of water. We made eye contact and both gave a smile and head nod. He strolled over.

"How was the hike?" he asked.

"It could not have been more beautiful. I spent a lot of time at the lake enjoying the reflection of the mountains and trees. It was like a painting," I said.

"Van Gogh couldn't have painted it better," Vincent said and winked.

I nodded.

"What's the plan for the afternoon?" he asked.

"Unfortunately, my friends aren't able to make the trip. I'm trying to decide whether I should stay or head back home."

"Well, if you already took the time off for yourself, why not make the most of it?"

I thanked Vincent and off he went.

I thought about what Vincent had said, and I didn't disagree. I needed this time. I decided to rethink my hikes and invest my energy in longer, more difficult hikes. I would stretch myself both mentally and physically over the next four days. Maybe the starburst jasper plaque was a message to me from the universe – another sign that my mom was always with me in spirit.

I got up from lunch and looked around at all the people at the lodge. There were many families having fun and connecting. My eye was drawn to a father and son playing chess – a game I hadn't played in a while. It made me reminisce about how much I loved that game, the strategy, and the intellectual stimulation. I headed back to the cabin to relax for a bit.

When evening was upon me, I made my way to see Grayce and tell her about my day. The sun was just setting, and she was setting up the telescopes. I shared with her about my hike, the reflections, and how the starburst jasper at the end had helped me recognize such a profound relationship between her conversation, my hike, and the mind, body, and soul connection. I also explained that I did a lot of reflecting and recognized that sometimes I let the ripples in life cause such huge disturbances that it impacted what I saw and how I acted.

She smiled. "It seems everything ties back to the stars."

"What do you mean?" I asked.

"Your comments on starburst jasper are so aligned to the universe. Let me show you something." She pointed at a group of stars in the sky. "You see the Big Dipper?"

I nodded.

"There's another constellation built off the Big Dipper. The entire constellation is Ursa Major, or the Big Bear. It's the third-largest constellation in the sky and the largest constellation in the Northern Hemisphere."

She pointed again to the sky to show all the points in Ursa Major. "Astronomers discovered a starburst galaxy in Ursa Major called Messier 82 or the Cigar Galaxy because with a telescope it looks like a rod of light near the constellation. So when you mentioned starburst jasper, it reminded me about the importance of these starburst galaxies."

"What are they?" I said.

"Starburst galaxies are undergoing very fast rates of star formation and rebirth. They're typically formed when they interact or collide with other nearby galaxies. It's an interesting metaphor for what we deal with in life. Sometimes we need a little bit of interaction with someone or something that provides the resources needed to develop new stars in our own personal galaxy," she said, smiling.

"That's really insightful, Grayce." Jokingly, I said, "I probably need to interact and collide with something so I can go through some rapid star formation myself."

"Don't we all?" she responded. "No one can grow without the right environment to produce new stars in their life. Sometimes it takes some productive conflict and sharing resources for something new to emerge. The more people and resources that you can Be Proximal with, the more rapid your personal growth and development will be."

She looked up at the stars for a moment and added, "One of my mentors taught me that you can't learn anything new until you're open enough to forget everything you think you know."

I thanked Grayce again and returned to my cabin for the evening. I sat on the edge of my bed and googled some starburst galaxy images. They were amazing. Then I went to the park's website, scrolled through the distances and difficulty levels of the different hiking trails, and read some of the reviews. I wanted to do a great hike tomorrow that would challenge me. I noticed the Butterfly Grove Trail about an hour's drive from the lodge. The reviews said the trail was lined with large sequoias and had a blend of shade and sun. All the reviews were favorable except for a single one-star review that complained the person hadn't seen a single butterfly, but I was not necessarily there to see butterflies. The hike would take about four hours, and I decided I would need to get to the Butterfly Grove Trail by 7:30 a.m. to beat the morning hiking crowd. I set the alarm for 6:00 a.m.

I opened my journal and tried to capture some of my discoveries from the day.

Be Brilliant

Tuesday 10:05 p.m.
A small disturbance in the lake can change the way things look. These disturbances impact so much more than the initial ripples caused by a rock thrown into them. Reflection Lake made me think about how this relates to life. Little things can cause such stress and impact so much. These things can have a ripple effect and cause chaos, yet despite disturbing the beautiful reflections, the ripples had their own beauty.

Was there something beautiful in the disturbance of our group trip?

There is something special in the mind–body connection of starburst jasper and starburst galaxies. Grayce said that no one can grow without the right environment to produce new stars in their life. Sometimes it takes some productive conflict and sharing resources for something new to emerge. The more people and resources that you can be proximal with, the more rapid your personal growth and development will be. I am questioning Grayce's advice here. Is there such a thing as productive conflict? Weird.

One of my mentors always talked about unlearning being as important as learning. When Grayce said, "You can't learn anything new until you are open enough to forget everything you think you know," it made me think of her. Am I open? What do I know?

Like last night, I looked at some of the reflections and wanted to capture something that really resonated. I want to put a star next to that last point. I love to learn, but can I unlearn?

What were your Be Brilliant key learnings?

_____

_____

_____

_____

_____

_____

_____

CHAPTER 5

*Star*light

I arrived at the base of the Butterfly Grove Trail and managed to find a parking spot. For some reason, I had butterflies in my stomach. I wasn't nervous about the hike, but I was feeling a bit anxious that my group trip had turned out to be the adventures of the lone wolf. I guess that's life, though. My mom always told me to expect the unexpected and I would never be disappointed. Sometimes that's easier said than done.

I sat in my truck and opened Instagram to post some of my pictures from yesterday while thinking about Vincent's advice to make the most of this unexpected turn of events. As long as I was here, I needed to embrace the time. As I scrolled through my IG feed, I saw that a childhood friend had shared a quote on her page: "You can't learn anything new until you are open enough to forget everything you think you know." I scrolled back and read it again.

This was the same quote Grayce had shared with me the previous night. I hadn't really thought about it too much, but now I was wondering if someone was trying to tell me something. I laughed at the serendipity and got out of my truck.

I looked up and noticed that the sky was dark, but my weather app showed only a 15% chance of rain. The strong scent of the sequoia trees hit me, and an immediate sense of calm came over me. I closed my eyes and took a deep breath, absorbing the earthy aroma. My mind shifted to the starburst jasper I'd read about yesterday on the Reflection Lake trail, and I appreciated the interconnected feeling of mind and body. It was a good reminder to be present with myself.

I took another long inhale as I walked into the trailhead and up the big boardwalk. I followed the twisting and turning route to some wooden stairs. A little further on, I stopped to take a few pictures of a mule deer that was peeking out from behind a fallen tree. As I crossed a park road to continue to the trail on the other side, a few sporadic raindrops pelted my head. I opened my weather app and it looked like a quick storm would be passing through, so I took it as an opportunity to test the poncho that Tye had recommended for all of us.

I propped my backpack on a picnic table, dug out my snug pack poncho, and proactively threw it on before the rain drops multiplied. I sent a selfie to my friends, captioned, "Lone wolf will not be the wet wolf." I knew they would get a kick out of how ridiculous the poncho looked on me. Their colorful responses had us all laughing.

I started walking, still chuckling at our group chat, and heard a voice from behind me. "Sir, I think this fell out of your bag back there." A woman handed me a brown stone with swirls of yellows and greens ribboned through the middle.

"No," I replied, "that doesn't belong to me, but it's a cool-looking stone. It looks like it's yours now."

She smiled as she cupped the stone in her hand and told me to enjoy the hike.

This place was full of good energy. Just as I finished that thought, the sparse rain drops turned into a steady torrent and I shook my head, reminding myself to soak it up – literally.

It was no wonder Tye had recommended this poncho; I felt like a duck as the water just rolled off me, leaving my clothes completely dry. The smell of the air was now a mixture of sequoias and fresh rain. I took another deep inhale, closed my eyes, and enjoyed a profound sense of peace. I almost felt lighter.

I came upon a place where the path passed right through the middle of an amazing tree whose trunk was wider than a street. This trail was supposed to include a tree that was actually called a telescope tree, but I was pretty sure this wasn't it. I reviewed my map more closely and realized I was on a different trail than I'd planned.

"You look like you're lost," a soft voice said from behind me. I turned to see a young woman who appeared to be in her early to mid-20s. If there was such thing as a stylish hiker, she was it.

"I think I took a wrong turn somewhere. I was trying to find the telescope tree," I explained.

"Oh, yes, the telescope tree is that way," she said, pointing to my left.

"Ah! I was so captivated by the sight of this tree right here," I said, "I must have missed the turn."

"Oh, this tree is incredible," she said. "It's called the tunnel tree. Sometimes I just stand under it and think about the beauty of nature. This is my zen hike. I live in the area and come here to clear my mind and recenter myself. I'm headed to the telescope tree now. Would you like to join me?"

"Are you sure? I don't want to infringe on your zen time."

She smiled and motioned for me to walk with her. Despite my commitment to do this solo without my friends, it was nice to have some company. The air now smelled like a potpourri of fresh rain, cedar, and essential oils. It reminded me of the smell of a local spa that ordered wine from me.

"My name is Emme. What's yours?"

"Jack. Thanks for redirecting me, Emme. This place almost doesn't feel real." I smiled through the rain and said, "You know, I feel unusually calm despite getting lost."

"Now you know why this is my zen place, Jack. There is nothing else like it for me."

When we arrived at the telescope tree, I was in awe. The telescope tree was everything I'd read and more. I walked inside the giant trunk and gazed up at the hollow tree inside to see the sky. Some ants and other bugs crawled on the wood inside of the tree, but my eyes fixed upon a small scorpion, something that I'd never seen in real life before. I never wanted to leave.

Emme and I continued on the trail together. As we reached the highest point of the hike, she told me we were at 6,853 feet. The views of the sky took my breath away. We both stood there in silence and enjoyed the slow breeze from across the open valley.

I don't know how long we had been standing there when I heard Emme say, "Make a wish."

I tilted my head inquisitively.

She followed with, "It's 11:11. Make a wish."

I closed my eyes for a long moment, breathed in the mountain air, and made my wish.

Hours felt like minutes in the hike down the mountain. Between the wildlife and the feeling of the sequoia canopy overhead, the experience felt surreal. As we neared the end of the trail, Emme called me over to a wooden sign.

"Jack, come read this," Emme said.

The sign read:

Of all the jasper stones, butterfly jaspers have an additional metaphysical element. Butterfly Grove Trail is named after this stone because this trail helps ground you. Butterfly jaspers are said to enable a feeling of being free and light and help imagination soar to new heights. Butterfly jaspers allow you to feel your emotions and deal with any challenges life throws your way. Butterfly jaspers clear the air and help you understand emotions while staying true to who you are as a person.

Emme pulled a stone out of her pocket and handed it to me. "Here, take this with you on your journey to keep you grounded as you soar to new heights."

It resembled the beautiful stone the other woman had thought I lost this morning. "Wow, I don't know what to say. Thank you."

"It's one of my favorite stones. This is butterfly jasper and your reminder to visit this trail again someday. I have to run now. It was a gift to spend time with you, Jack."

"Bye, Emme. It was so great that our paths crossed. Thank you again," I said as I held up the stone.

I took some pictures of the sign and checked my watch. The four-hour hike had turned into five hours because of all my stops and reflective moments. I would get back to the lodge just in time to grab a late lunch and relax. Of course, I couldn't wait to see Grayce and tell her about the butterfly jasper and its properties to ground you to you stay true to who you are. It seemed to me that Grayce had already done this in her life. She had freed herself from her daily routine and let her imagination soar by doing something she loved.

When I arrived back at the lodge, I grabbed a bite to eat. I saw the same dad and boy playing chess again in the lobby. I wanted to play a game myself but I was hesitant to approach because it looked like a lot of pieces were still on the board and they could be there a while. I made a personal commitment right then and there to connect with someone at the park who liked chess. Perhaps tomorrow would be the perfect time to play the game that I loved and had been missing.

I went back to the cabin, pulled out my journal, and wrote the information on butterfly jasper and a couple of other aha moments from the hike.

I went to the core of learning and growth around 8:00 for stargazing. A few people were looking at the stars and listening to Grayce. I could see her pointing and happily discussing the universe with her infectious energy. I waited so I could ensure the other viewers had her full attention. And perhaps more selfishly, I also wanted to see what she'd show me tonight after they were done.

When the crowd cleared, I walked over.

"Hi, Grayce," I said.

"Hello, Jack. How was the hiking today?"

"It was great! I went to Butterfly Grove Trail. It was a beautiful hike."

"Oh, tell me about it." she said.

I explained my experiences and learnings from the trail. I mentioned some of the wildlife and the fact that I had even seen a scorpion.

A family came over to talk to Grayce, so I stepped aside as she showed them the stars. I listened to how she explained the brightness of the stars and how they illuminate the night individually, but together they create beautiful images.

When the family left, I walked back over.

"You didn't have to walk away," she said.

"No worries," I said.

"Okay, so did I hear you say you saw a scorpion? That's pretty rare!" she exclaimed.

"I know. It was cool. Also, the end of the trail had a really inspirational message regarding butterfly jasper. Yesterday was starburst jasper and today butterfly," I laughed.

"So what does butterfly jasper do?" she asked.

"It grounds us, helps us manage emotions, and provides us the ability to feel and navigate emotions for whatever comes our way. I thought of you because you were able to ground yourself right here in the core of learning and growth. You stayed true to who you are and are doing something you love."

She liked that. "That's true! I love what I do. I'll have to get some butterfly jasper for the house. So tell me, why did you choose Butterfly Grove Trail?"

"Yesterday, you were talking about how the environment needed to be right and the conditions required for new stars to form. The butterfly seems much the same way to me. It starts as one thing and through various stages of its life it transforms to something that supports the growth and life of all things around you.

Butterflies are pollinators, so when I saw the trail name, it just felt right," I said.

"Yes, butterflies are certainly pollinators. I have a friend, Catherine, who says people are also pollinators and can spread positive growth and development in their world, too."

I nodded. "That makes a lot of sense."

Suddenly, Grayce's face lit up. "Hey! You mentioned you did the Butterfly Grove Trail and you saw a scorpion. You want to see something really cool?" She pointed to the moon and then Mars on the horizon and continued. "People often mistakenly think the star Antares is Mars because of its red tone, but it's actually how we can find the constellation Scorpio in the southern sky."

She pointed to all the stars that formed Scorpio's outline. At first it was hard to grasp, but as she explained it more I could start to make out the shape. Then Grayce pulled out her phone and showed me an amazing photo of a butterfly of stars flying though space.

"This is the Butterly Nebula," she explained. "It can only really be seen by advanced telescopes like Hubble, but it's remarkable. It extends right off Scorpio's tail. You know, Scorpios are passionate, independent, and not afraid to blaze their own trail, much like you did today, Jack. Are you a Scorpio?"

"No, I'm a Cancer."

"Me too!" exclaimed Grayce. "Anyway, as I was saying, this beautiful Butterfly Nebula is ironically in the Scorpio's most dangerous feature, its tail. Many people try to avoid dangerous, risky situations where there is conflict or fear of failure, but looking at this nebula is a wonderful example of how not avoiding these challenging situations and taking risks can help illuminate something you otherwise might not see. I'm not saying to go out and seek out real danger, but putting yourself in situations where there is discomfort, anxiety, and fear leads to things you may never realize."

"That's why I'm trying some more challenging hikes this week. And each day I'm learning something new," I replied.

"Exactly. It's just like the butterfly effect. Sometimes a small, seemingly trivial event may ultimately result in something with much larger consequences. I think this is a choose-your-lens moment. Often, we tend to look at the little things we do and the negative effects they can have on something. But our ecosystems are vastly complex and nebulous, so we need to look at the butterfly effect as a catalyst for meaningful change. Instead of looking at the negative effects of things we do in our environment, we can look at all the trivial things we do and the massive impact they can have in creating wonderful changes."

When I returned to my cabin, I opened the park's app to find a trail for the next day. About a 45-minute drive away was a hike that jumped out at me, with stunning views of lakes. This out-and-back-trail was a nice 10-mile moderately difficult hike. I figured I would get an early start and try to be at the parking lot around 7 a.m. Likely, it would take a good six hours to complete the hike and another hour to drive home.

Once I was at the cabin, I opened my journal and stared at the pages. In just two days I had a few pages full of notes from my conversations with Grayce and my aha moments from the hikes.

Be Brilliant

Wednesday 9:55 p.m.

It's amazing to me that I hiked with a perfect stranger today! Strangely, Emme never felt like a stranger. She was both energizing and calming at the same time. I keep thinking about the view from the telescope tree and the feeling of being at 6,853 feet. The view was crisp, exhilarating, and will be forever imprinted in my mind. I am using this as a timestamp – at 11:11 a.m. on this Wednesday morning, I was standing at 6,853 feet when I made my wish. I wonder if it will come true.

I realize that many things in life are interrelated and interconnected. I reread what I wrote last night after my experience at Reflection Lake. It's the little things in life that mean so much – the ripples, the environment being right, our mind/body connection. The butterfly is so representative of this because it starts as one thing, and through various stages of its life, it transforms to something different that supports growth and life. The transformation may seem insignificant if you don't have the lens to see it right. I am realizing that this can happen to people, too. Am I transforming? What does that even mean?

I am holding my butterfly jasper stone from Emme in one hand and writing this excerpt with the other. The energy of the stone makes me feel grounded. I'm wondering if that is because I read this on the trail sign; I may be experiencing recency bias, but regardless, I kinda like it. If this stone will help me soar to new heights, where do I want to go? How can I stay true to who I am? Who am I anyway? As I write, I realize I have more questions than answers. But it feels good.

What were your Be Brilliant key learnings?

_____

_____

_____

_____

_____

_____

_____

_____

CHAPTER
6

Costar

"Welcome to Beehive Meadow Trail," read the sign at the entrance to the hike. I parked my truck near the sign and let my device finish playing the Beatles' "Here Comes the Sun." It set the perfect vibe for tackling this hike.

The description of the trailhead said that Beehive Meadow Trail started off by a beautiful reservoir, which was reminiscent of my first hike to Reflection Lake, where the ripples brought both disturbance and beauty to the water. It was a switchback trail, so I would end up right here from a different part of the trail. I grabbed my gear and started along the narrow clay path. The elevation gain was about 2,700 feet, so I knew it would be a nice workout.

About two miles into the hike, I saw a sign. It looked like this was the other entrance or exit from the switchback. I also noticed a large granite object and an information board. I was tempted to read it now before the hike, but I resisted the urge. I wanted to stay quiet with my own thoughts and consider some of the things I had already learned on the trip. I had also brought my journal with me, so I could capture any notes or thoughts I had.

As I approached the reservoir, I saw its large granite walls shimmering in the sunlight as the water flowed down, as if the walls were crying tears of joy. I stopped to take some pictures, even though my pictures never seemed to do justice to the natural beauty when I looked at them later in my room.

After two more hours of hiking and stopping along the many vistas for some reflective moments, I reached a tunnel with a sign that said, "Trail Meadows This Way." I followed the tunnel, which took me to the opposite side of the reservoir. My GPS told me I was on the western side.

After navigating many trails and switchbacks, I stopped at a vista along the shaded path. The smell of pines permeated the air. The trail hadn't been too busy until now, but there seemed to be a lot more foot traffic in this area. Up ahead I could see there was another trail that merged with this one. It seemed everyone was getting ready to go down that trail.

The trees were dense, but there was a gap where I could make out the Sierra Nevadas in the distance. I stood at the edge of the vista and studied the mountains.

I suddenly heard a crunching sound behind me and turned around. Sure enough, a guy was standing there all decked out in camping gear and eating an apple. He had a rolled-up tent on top of his backpack and a long beard. He nodded at me and smiled.

"Some view, huh?" he said.

"It's okay. I'm sure there are much better ones up ahead. This one's kind of obstructed, but shady, so I'm enjoying it."

"Any view from up here, obstructed or not, is certainly pristine. You heading to Beehive Meadow?" he asked.

"I am. It sounds like a great spot."

"I do this trail often for that very reason. The natural wildflowers bring all sorts of great pollinators out into the meadow. It's certainly a sight to see. But the view you have now is one of my favorites. Look out there. That mountain range is home to some of the largest trees in the world, the sequoias, but there's something even more special about them," he said as he pointed to the Sierra Nevadas.

"What's that?" I asked curiously. Being from California, I was well aware that it was home to three renowned parks including the sequoias, but I wasn't sure where he was going with this.

"Each peak and sequoia on this mountain alone is majestic in its own right, but when they all work together, they're so much more beautiful. It's like when you watch a movie. One actor might be a star, but it's all the costars who bring the movie together. There is something beautiful about togetherness."

"I see what you mean. They're also like the stars in a constellation," I said.

"Exactly! That's the perfect way of putting it. From what I understand, this mountainous region you're peering at right now is still growing. Even though they are expanding very slowly, they continue to stretch upwards and outwards. The shape of the mountains you see today will one day look completely different, but we will never be able to really tell because of the mountain's vastness. They're not so different from us in that way. Even small incremental changes can make a difference in the way we grow, but to those around us, those small changes sometimes may go unnoticed in the short term. That's okay, though. We're still growing."

"Wow, that's interesting. Hey, I didn't catch your name."

"My name is Daniel."

"I'm Jack." As we shook hands, I asked, "So what makes the mountains grow?"

"It's said that this mountain range lives on a fault line and tectonic plate activity is always occurring. The movement of those plates underneath the surface is what keeps the expansion of these mountains going, just like the trees continue to grow each year. The reason I love this spot is because it's like having my own personal movie of nature. The mountain range and the sequoias are the perfect costars. Alone, I don't think one peak and one tree would have the same impact. It's hard for one star to carry the whole show. Having costars is something we all need in our own personal story."

"Thanks, Daniel. You've given me a whole new perspective on things. I've really enjoyed the conversation, but I guess I'd better be getting on with my hike."

"Well, Jack, I don't want to keep you. Nice meeting you," he said.

As he walked down the trail, I pulled out my journal. I wanted to take a few notes on what he said. Who were my costars? Did I have any?

I made my way up the trail until I came to Beehive Meadow. It was jaw dropping; the wildflowers and the panoramic views from here were stunning. The mountains in the background were so much clearer from here and looked more massive. I could see the bees all around doing their jobs, unconcerned with the hikers playing in the meadow. I took a moment to capture some images and created a story on Instagram. This was by far the best hike yet.

After a while I took the next trail down to the trailhead. It was a nice two-and-a-half-hour hike back but mostly downhill, so my focus was on not blowing out a knee. I reflected on the conversation with Daniel a little bit. He had made some interesting points about how small changes might not be immediately visible to others and even over time people might not see a huge difference in the ways things look, but even small changes can help things grow. I feel this way sometimes in my life. I think I'm doing something to grow, and though it might seem to go unnoticed, I know I'm growing. Maybe one day all those small changes I'm making to improve myself will result in something that looks completely different. I already feel there will be a lot of growth coming from this trip.

As I came to the trailhead, I could see that large stone and information sign that I'd noticed earlier. I was excited to read what it said. I took some pictures of the stone and sign and began to read.

Bumblebee jasper helps us to examine opportunities that exist for us to stay positive during a time when the journey may be frustrating. The goal of the bumblebee jasper is to help us to see the silver linings, demonstrate a growth mindset, and enjoy the life we have. Bumblebee jasper is a happy stone of courage. It brings to light that the actual truth about us as individuals and our current situation is far more positive than we've been led to believe. The stone encourages people to enjoy our life more and to surround ourselves with beauty. Bumblebee jasper inspires us to be more confident and rely on personal ability much more, to be self-confident while also being generous with our love and attention. The stone's properties help us to stop worrying about how other people view us in this world and instead concentrate on how we can be the best version of ourselves.

When I sat in my truck, I thought about the profoundness of what I'd learned on today's hike.

Experts say there can be a recency bias effect in life; I was being so reflective on these hikes, and I wondered if the messages were a result of that. Everything seemed to resonate at the right time. I thought it would be interesting to hear Grayce's thoughts on this. I was pretty confident there was no Bee zodiac symbol or constellation, so I was interested to learn the stone–star connection on this one.

I turned the Beatles' "Here Comes the Sun" back on, opened my journal, and quickly jotted down my thoughts while they were still fresh in my mind.

Be Brilliant

Thursday 1:30 p.m.

Today I learned that bumblebee jasper is a stone that helps us to stay positive during a time when our journey may be frustrating. Do I see the silver linings in my life? Do I enjoy the life I have? Do I see the beauty around me? Am I being the best version of me? I have never thought of these questions before. Sometimes I can have a bad attitude when things don't go my way. I wonder if I'm missing the learning moments. Hmm.

I loved how Daniel shared his view of the sequoias and the mountain together. He made me see the single sequoias standing alone and suddenly I saw them differently. He was right; one tree didn't have the same impact as the collection of the peaks and trees together. There is something beautiful about togetherness. Are Antonio and Tye my costars? Who the heck are my costars in life? My mind is racing. . . .

What were your Be Brilliant key learnings?

_____

_____

_____

_____

_____

_____

_____

_____

CHAPTER 7

Super*star*

On my drive back from Beehive Meadow Trail, I stopped at the visitors center. The snacks I had taken on the hike had held me over, but I needed another quick snack to keep me going. The hike had been mentally, physically, and spiritually uplifting and empowering, but I could feel I was in a calorie deficit. In fact I was craving one of the red, white, and blue rocket pops that I had seen in the freezer there on the first day, so I got one to tide me over for the moment.

I headed back to the cabin, unpacked my hiking gear, and sat on the porch outside. It was the first time I'd ventured out there, and it was quite peaceful. I saw lots of small animals like squirrels and chipmunks. I even saw a deer as it was running by. It was so relaxing in the rocking chair that I didn't want to get up, but the sugar rush from the rocket pop was going to wear off soon, and I needed some real food.

I took a quick shower and headed up to the lodge for a late lunch around 4:30. The café offered different types of sandwiches, soups, and salads. As I stood in line my eyes were bouncing all around, because I was fond of people watching. The crowd at the sundry shop was full of hikers and families, all enjoying a quick break.

After I grabbed my food, I found a table to sit down and eat. Across the way I saw a boy sitting by the chessboards. He was alone and chatting on his phone, and the board was set up. I was so tired, but it seemed the kid was looking for a game. Something pulled me over there. Maybe it was my love for chess, my curiosity, or just my wanting to make sure the boy was okay. I finished my food, tossed the recycling and trash in the appropriate bins, took my last swig of water, and walked over to the chessboard.

As I approached, I could see the boy was wearing sunglasses inside and had wavy light brown hair. He looked to be in his late teens or early 20s, but it was hard to tell for sure. When I arrived at the table, I noticed his sunglasses had a strap to hold them in place on his head.

"Hi, I'm Jack," I said. "You looking for a game?"

The boy looked up. "Hi, I'm Geo. Sure, I have time for a game. Do you play a lot?"

"Honestly, I used to love to play. But I haven't played in a very long time. You seem like you play a lot. I think I've seen you playing every day."

"My dad and I play a lot," Geo said. "It's something we both love to do and it gives us some bonding time."

"Alright, let's do this," I said.

I sat down at the table. Since I had the white chess pieces, I made the first move. Geo kept his sunglasses on, which I thought was interesting. Maybe he didn't want to give any tells with his eyes.

We exchanged moves for 10 minutes. Geo was way better than me and was capturing my pieces with ease. He always seemed to be one step ahead.

"Check," Geo said as he moved his rook into position. I could see him stoically anticipating how I was going to get out of check so he could pounce on me.

I moved my king into one of the two spots I could go.

He quickly moved his knight. "Checkmate," he declared. "Good game."

I was simultaneously impressed and a bit embarrassed. "Wow. That was fast. Great game, Geo."

"You said you hadn't played in a while," Geo said. "It takes some time to knock the rust off. Do you want to play again?"

He began setting up the board in anticipation that I would say yes. Although I was tired, I felt like I needed to try and redeem myself.

"Sure," I said. "Thanks for the opportunity. How long have you been playing?"

"I've been playing since I was 5 years old, so about 14 years. I came to love the game, the strategy, and how each piece is unique in how it can move and has a defined responsibility, but all the pieces working together become an amazing force of teamwork."

"Geo, that is pretty profound."

He nodded. "My dad says that we're each chess pieces in our own way. We have a path that has been chosen for us and we can't deviate from it. We need to work within the confines of our abilities and can still make an impact."

I actually kind of disagreed with his dad's statement but I didn't really know the kid, so I thought it would be inappropriate to comment. Instead, I just nodded.

"Okay, your move Geo," I said.

This game lasted a little longer but not by much. Geo beat me swiftly again. I could see him crack a smile.

"Good game!"

"Geo, are you hustling people again?" a voice asked.

I turned around and saw Geo's father. I stood up and introduced myself.

"Geo is an awesome chess player," I said.

"He certainly is. He really has a firm grasp of the strategy and the nuances of the game. He competes and is ranked as one of the top chess players in the nation. He basically goes to school and plays chess."

"That's awesome. Congrats, Geo," I said.

Geo looked up and nodded. In his quiet voice he said, "Thanks, not much else to do."

His father ignored the comment so I didn't ask Geo to elaborate, but we continued to talk about the park and what their plans were for the week. I was curious about Geo's sunglasses, so I asked his father. He shared that Geo had a rare disease that severely restricted his vision, caused light sensitivity, and resulted in some other degenerative conditions, but that he was actually doing great.

I said I would make sure to keep Geo in my thoughts, which he appreciated.

"Geo, I've got to hit the road, but I want one more crack at you the next time I see you. I want to beat the Superstar," I said.

"Name the time and place." He smiled.

We all said goodbye, and I headed back to the cabin. It was about 6:30 p.m. I decided to take a quick nap before going to see Grayce. Each day I was more excited to experience her profound way of connecting the stars to the rocks that I found on my hikes. The parallels were fascinating. The 10-mile hike today had been exhausting, and the dinner I had just eaten was giving me a food coma. I set my alarm for 8:30 p.m. and figured I would go see Grayce around sunset. My head hit the pillow and I dozed off to recharge.

CHAPTER
8

Be*star*red

I woke up from my nap to the sound of my alarm, and honestly my excitement prior to the nap had shifted to wanting to just sleep. Nevertheless, I freshened up, got changed, and hopped in the truck to drive down to see Grayce at the telescopes. Beehive Meadow Trail was one of my favorite hikes to date. There were so many scenic spots and learning moments. I figured I would show Grayce what I had learned about the bumblebee jasper and see if there were any celestial connections. That was what I appreciated most – even though she was an amateur astronomer, she knew how to make connections and learning moments for me. She seemed to have a gift as a storyteller, too.

Grayce was the only person at the telescopes when I arrived, and I could see the soft glow of her cell phone on her face. She was probably doing what most people do while waiting around: checking social media and catching up on the latest happenings.

She gave a friendly wave when she saw me approaching. "Good evening, Jack! How was the hike today?"

"Oh, it was a very busy day," I replied.

Her brow furrowed. "Busy? I don't use that word, Jack. I use the word *full*. The word *busy* casts us and the people around us in a negative light. It makes people think we have no time for them. On the other hand, the word *full* primes us to gather and share the goodness from the day. Of course, this is just one woman's perspective."

I smiled. "I guess my day was full then."

"So where did you hike today?"

I told her all about my 10-mile hike along Beehive Meadow Trail and showed her my phone. She looked at the message about bumblebee jasper from the picture I took and read it out loud.

"Bumblebee jasper helps us to examine opportunities that exist for us to stay positive during a time when the journey may be frustrating. The goal of the bumblebee jasper is to help us to see the silver linings, demonstrate a growth-mindset, and enjoy the life we have. Bumblebee jasper is a happy stone of courage. It brings to light that the actual truth about us as individuals and our current situation is far more positive than we've been led to believe. The stone encourages people to enjoy our life more and to surround ourselves with beauty. Bumblebee jasper inspires us to be more confident and rely on personal ability much more, to be self-confident while also being generous with our love and attention. The stone's properties help us to stop worrying about how other people view us in this world and instead concentrate on how we can be the best version of ourselves."

"That's beautiful," she said. "Jack, we haven't even talked about you or this vineyard you own. It seems like the bumblebee jasper is speaking to you. Tell me about it. I could feel your energy when you handed me this photo, like this message really resonated with you."

I explained how I had partnered with my uncle on his vineyard after my career as a teacher, thinking it would be my next career journey. The unexpected loss of my aunt had resulted in my uncle wanting to sell the vineyard. My attempt to achieve the seemingly impossible goal of running the vineyard and helping its brand grow had been an ongoing challenge. Lately I had been feeling like I was on a journey that didn't seem like it was going to pan out. I was trying to figure things out and be more self-reliant on my abilities to contribute to the vineyard's success.

She was actively listening – her eyes were fixed on me, and her body language demonstrated care and concern.

"I can tell that was uncomfortable for you to share, Jack. You seem very private. You don't demonstrate a whole lot of vulnerability, do you?"

"I'm typically a pretty private person, but I was happy to tell you my story."

"Well, maybe it's the way you said it, Jack. Sometimes the way we say things to people might come out a little differently than what we intend, so I'm happy you got a little vulnerable," she responded. After a brief moment, she continued, "So what did you think of the bumblebee jasper message?"

"It really resonated with me. I'm doing something that feels very hard and trying to achieve these impossible goals of running the vineyard alone. You know, I met a guy on the trail who pointed out how the mountains and trees seem so much more significant when they're together than when they're alone. They're costars in the imagery they make. I thought it was interesting and made sense. The message is certainly a positive one."

Grayce nodded. "That's great advice, Jack. Costars are really important in your life. Reflecting on my interpretation of the sign, the bumblebee jasper does seem to bring courage and positivity. But there's one aspect of the message that I disagree with."

"Which part?"

"The part where people need to rely on their own personal ability. I think personal ability is important, but people need to shine bright, with costars, like the Beehive Cluster of stars."

I gave an "aha" as she threaded the costar comment so nicely.

"Speaking of clusters of stars, at this time of year the constellation of Cancer can be faintly seen in the western sky. . . ."

"That's my zodiac sign," I interjected.

"Do you know much about the meanings of the zodiac, or do you just know that Cancer is your sign?" she inquired.

"I just know it's my sign. I've never been much into astrology and haven't explored the depths of its meaning."

"Well, I totally understand that. But what's even more special, Jack, is that even though you don't know about what your sign means, you seem open to learning new things."

"I try to be. So what's so special about Cancers?" I asked.

"Well, I'm not actually an astrologer or a subject matter expect on the zodiac. I just know where to find things in the sky. What I can tell you is that Cancers are creative and resilient, they can always find pleasure in their own company and their own mind, and they can do special things. Just like you're doing on your hikes, Jack."

I nodded.

She continued, "It's been said that the emotional intelligence of Cancer is really remarkable, and they can quickly get to the heart of the issue. Turning the lens of the telescope inward is a challenge for them because that means they may get emotional, and those emotions may erupt unexpectedly. Another thing about Cancer is they expect other people to already know what's on their mind, which often causes frustration for Cancers. The greatest opportunity for people with this sign is to voice opinions and feelings even if it leads to some conflict. Do you erupt emotionally, Jack? You don't seem like the type."

"I think we all have moments of emotion, and I'm no different. Where is Cancer in the sky? Can you show me?"

A group of people came up to the telescopes. Grayce engaged with them for about 10 minutes, and it was now almost 9:30. I knew she needed to pack up, and I didn't want to keep her.

But when Grayce finished with the people, she resumed our conversation. She pointed to three bright stars in the western sky, explaining that the star Regulus and the stars Castor and Pollux, which are in the Gemini constellation, could help guide me to see Cancer.

I could see the stars she was talking about. She pointed halfway between Regulus and Castor and Pollux and asked if I could see the faint open cluster of stars.

I could not.

She reached into her bag and pulled out a pair of binoculars. She peered through the them at the sky and found what she was looking for. Then she handed the binoculars to me and helped me find the star cluster.

"Look at that loosely bound group of stars," she prompted. "That's a star cluster, and they were born together, Jack. This one is called the Beehive Cluster because it looks like a bunch of tiny bees swarming around a hive. It has the largest population of stars in the galaxy. The Beehive Cluster is important because it's how we find the faint constellation of Cancer."

She pointed to two faint stars above the Beehive Cluster and three below it that almost formed a triangle and told me, "That is Cancer, Jack."

"I can see it," I answered.

Grayce said, "When you stop to think about the messages on the trail signs, it's amazing how the small rocks and stones have such a connection to the stars. Remember, Jack, it's okay to be self-reliant, but sometimes to achieve big goals you may need a cluster of something bright in your life to reveal an image of how things should look and be. Just like the Beehive Cluster does for Cancer."

"It's fascinating how the Beehive Cluster, bumblebee jasper, and Cancer all connect," I said.

"A very important person in my life taught me that even something as small as the bee can have a profound impact on lighting up our life. We all have an opportunity to become a pollinator, like a bee. It's one of the greatest things we can do in life. This circle we're standing in here, the core of learning and growth, is one of the places that I pollinate others. Just like bees form a hive so they can pollinate everything around them, we also have an opportunity to create our own little Beehive Cluster; a collection of stars can Bestar your life and help illuminate the things you cannot see or are unwilling to see. Do you happen to have beehives on your vineyard, Jack"?

I shook my head no. But I recognized that the question might have been her way of pollinating and planting an idea, which was not so terrible.

Grayce started packing up. She told me she would be back the next day, and that she was looking forward to the weekend. I had yet to tip her, but she did have a little jar with stars on it that said, "Be Bright!" There was some money in there, presumably from tonight's visitors. I pulled out my wallet and found $17 in there. I threw it in the jar when she wasn't looking. Her words and inspirations were worth way more than $17, but it was all I had on me.

I went back to my cabin to reflect on the evening's aha moments. I opened my journal and looked at the pages. My insights were multiplying every day, as if my brain was working in a different way as I prioritized time to reflect.

Be Brilliant

Thursday 10:05 p.m.

Grayce mentioned our connection to the stars. I tended to prefer to do things myself, so I never thought of being self-reliant as a bad thing. As we looked at the little Beehive Cluster together, she said that a collection of stars can help illuminate the things we cannot or are unwilling to see. Maybe that's why I preferred to do things alone!

The bumblebee jasper helps us to stay positive, be brave, and enjoy life. And the Cancer sign is resilient and emotionally intelligent. If the Beehive Cluster is in the heart of Cancer and has more costars than any other cluster, what does that mean when I put everything together? Can I be happier and more resilient if I work with a larger group of stars in my own life?

What were your Be Brilliant key learnings?

_____

_____

_____

_____

_____

_____

_____

CHAPTER
9

Stargaze

The morning was quiet, and so was my mind as I drove to the trailhead. I was listening to the London Symphony Orchestra's *Marriage of Figaro*, which tended to have that effect on me ever since my college mentor taught me how classical music primes the brain for clarity and concentration. Among the many pearls of wisdom she had shared, this one really stuck with me, and to this day, the moment I hear classical music, an immediate sense of calm comes over me. It's like a Pavlov's dog experience. I felt myself smile as I thought about the impact she'd had on life. I wondered if she knew the extent of how much she had inspired some of her students.

I pulled into the parking area, found a spot, and sat in my truck listening to the music for what felt like an hour, but was really only the 11 minutes of the piece. *Wow, that feeling of inner-peace is powerful*, I thought to myself, recognizing another theme from this trip. I grabbed my backpack and my brand-new water shoes from the passenger seat. The shoes made me think of my friends and Antonio's strong push for his favorite brand of water shoes that we had all purchased. Given the three-hour time difference, I decided it wasn't too early to FaceTime with my friends.

"Hey, Jack," Tye said as his face appeared on my screen.

"Yo!" Antonio joined the call with his camera off, which was typical.

I got out of the truck and flipped my screen so I could slowly scan the area for my friends to get a taste of the breathtaking scenery.

"If you can't be here in person, at least you can get to experience it vicariously through me," I said as I walked toward my 10-mile adventure for the day. I held my water shoes up to the phone and told my friends that they'd be walking with me in spirit.

"In spirit is fine, but I wish we were there in person. Am I remembering correctly that we had White Wolf Trail scheduled for today?" Antonio asked.

"What a memory – if only it was that good in remembering people's names," I laughed.

"Seriously," Tye jumped in. "Remember that time when we ran into our most inspiring professor at homecoming and Antonio couldn't remember her name, so he called her the Classical Professor – to her face!"

"That's funny. I was just thinking of her this morning as I listened to my classical playlist."

Tye said, "Yeah, I remember she loved classical music. She was one of the best teachers. A real legend. What was her name, Antonio?"

"You think I still don't remember, don't you? You're wrong. Her name was Classical Professor!"

We all laughed, and I told them to check Instagram for the pics I would continue to post of this adventure. I put my phone in my pocket and stopped at a picnic table to do a quick bag check to ensure I had what I needed for the day. I took a quick selfie by the White Wolf Trail sign, popped in my earbuds, and headed toward the canopied trail ahead.

The shade and flat terrain of the first mile seemed fitting with the peace of my playlist. Everything felt still. I took a deep breath, absorbed the warm woodsy air, and let out a long exhale. The week had been interesting. I was unexpectedly spending time getting to know myself in ways I hadn't anticipated. But I also noticed a shift in how I saw the people around me, as if I had a newfound appreciation for the people in my life. What was happening to me?

As I emerged from the trees, a trail sign spotlighted by the sun spurred me to pull some sunscreen out of my bag. I put some on before entering the exposed terrain ahead, and followed the path to the first lake. When I arrived at the lake, I pulled out my earbuds. I hadn't seen anything in my research indicating any "quiet trails," but it certainly seemed very still here. I looked around and wondered if there were signs asking hikers to whisper. I wasn't sure if I was comfortable with no noise at all. But as I stared at the water and felt its peacefulness, I enjoyed how it quieted my mind.

Then I heard a familiar voice call me from the distance. It was Emme, looking stylish again with a baseball hat framing her face.

"Hey, stranger. What are you doing here?" I asked.

"I've had quite the week, so I came to visit the moonstone thinking stump for a few hours of peace. You want some company?"

"Moonstone thinking stump? Where's that?" I asked.

"It's about two miles that way." She pointed past the lake. "I can only join you to that point and then I have to turn back to get to work."

My first instinct was toward my preference to head out alone because that's what I had originally planned for the day. But I took a moment to reframe my thinking. This trip had me doing a lot of that.

"Sure, why not?" I couldn't believe the words that had just come out of my mouth. As an introvert, I didn't commonly hang out with people I didn't know very well, let alone spend hours on a hike together. And if Emme came here for peace, why wouldn't she also want to be alone? But that was that – we were going together.

"Woohoo, let's do this!" Emme yelled with her hands cupped around her mouth.

"Umm, if you're going to hike with me, we're not going to be *those people*," I said with air quotes. "You can hear a pin drop here."

Emme laughed and waved her hands in the air whispering "woohoo!" as we both walked around the lake. Her energy almost felt contagious. My morning had started very quietly but had quickly transitioned to a different energy. It was going to take me a while to process how I felt about it.

"So tell me about this moonstone that brought you here," I said to Emme as I captured a few photos of the view.

"Well, moonstone links with the zodiac signs Cancer, Scorpio, and Sagittarius. No, wait. Not Sagittarius, Libra. Anyway, that doesn't matter. What does matter is that it's also known as the wolf's eye," she declared as she pulled a crystal out of a little satin drawstring bag. She held it up to the sun and we both gazed on it. I admired the gentle yellow illumination that shone through the pearly white iridescence.

"It gets its name – moonstone – from its resemblance to the color and luminosity of the moon. My mentor gave this to me when I was struggling to find my purpose – my *why* as I like to call it now," she said as she snapped her fingers with a big smile.

I saw black spots for a moment from looking up toward the sun. I closed my eyes to let them readjust and took in a deep breath of the woodsy aroma. The warmth of the sun on my back prompted me to ask Emme if she minded the heat.

"Nope. I don't leave my house without sunscreen and a baseball hat, rain or shine," she said as she skipped down the narrow path that split the open meadow.

I shook my head and smiled at her positive energy as I picked up the pace to see what she was skipping toward. She stopped up ahead, breathlessly waving me over to the wooden sign she was leaning against.

The sign read:

> *Moonstone calms and relaxes the mind and body. It promotes inner peace that leads to emotional healing and spiritual connection. In grounding, moonstone clears scattered thoughts and induces the presence of the mind. It enables the person to live peacefully and accordingly to divine purpose.*

She opened her hand, revealing the moonstone. She handed it to me.

"You can't have this one, Jack, but I want you to hold it while I tell you a story."

The stone felt warm in my hand as I rubbed my fingers over it. Emme walked over to a couple of tree stumps that looked naturally staged for deep conversation.

She sat on a stump and told me, "Have a seat, Jack."

"Is this the moonstone thinking stump?" I asked as I sat on the tree stump next to her, continuing to fidget with the moonstone in my hand.

"That's right. So you're probably curious about my mentor and finding my *why* and everything in between, right, Jack?"

Her question made me reflect for a minute that this was not a strength of mine. While I cared about people, it didn't always come naturally for me to ask deeper and more personal questions. I was now wondering whether I might have offended Emme because I had unintentionally dismissed her comment earlier and focused on my eyes on readjusting from looking at the sun. I was grateful she prompted me to go back to her story, though, because I was curious. I needed to work on that. . . .

"Tell me," I said.

"Do you have any mentors?" she asked.

"Yes. It's funny you ask because I was just thinking about one of my mentors while listening to some classical music this morning that she'd introduced me to. She really had a profound impact on my life."

"Does she know that?" Emme asked.

"Years ago, I told her, but I'm not great at staying in touch with people."

"When you leave here today, Jack, I want you to email your mentor the link for the song that made you think of her, with a little expression of gratitude to go with it. Okay?"

"Sure," I said.

"So back to my moonstone story. When I was in college, my mentor always called me a lone wolf because asking for help wasn't one of my strong suits. In my senior year I was enrolled in her organizational behavior and leadership class, and when we were learning about what an organization's mission means, we were asked to first think about our personal purpose. This was the first time in my life that I was asked to think about a company's purpose, let alone my own purpose. The exercise ended up opening floodgates to some things I experienced in my childhood that made me somewhat fixed in my thinking." She looked up. "You still with me, Jack?"

"Yes, so how did the moonstone factor in?" I asked.

"I promise to make my long story as short as I can, but a story is no good without the details." She tilted her head and laughed, then proceeded with her story. "I struggled so much with this assignment that I ended up visiting my professor during office hours quite frequently to find answers. She unexpectedly became a source of light for me. When I showed up for one of our meetings, my chair had a moonstone in this little satin bag."

I looked down at the moonstone in my hand.

"That's right. That's the very moonstone she gave me. It came with a little note that she had handwritten for me that said, 'Sometimes in the dark we need the light of the moon to illuminate the path forward. Different people in your life will serve as your moon if you allow them.'"

"Wow. That's some gift," I said softly.

"It really was. She encouraged me to hold the moonstone during my morning yoga practice. It was in that moment that she asked me to consider who was part of *my pack*. At the time, I couldn't answer her. The good news is I have been building my pack ever since that day."

"I love this story on so many levels. I'm so grateful you shared this with me, Emme."

She handed me her phone, and I saw the "Create a New Contact" screen facing me.

"Jack, can we stay in touch?" she asked.

"I'd like that, Emme." I added my contact information in her phone.

Before Emme left to head to work, we exchanged a quick hug, which was another unusual thing for me to do with people I wasn't close to, but I was leaning in to everything that was new on this trip. The wheels were turning in my head as I continued up the trail, weaving in and out of canopied sequoia sections and open terrain. I felt so much peace inside.

My quads and glutes were sore today, so I found a hiking stick to ease the burn. But it was a "hurts so good" feeling that I actually enjoyed. My thoughts were interrupted by the sound of birds flying through the trees. Despite my fear of birds from a childhood experience with pet parakeets, I enjoyed watching them soar from afar. I felt connected to the freeing feeling of flying, especially after this week. I just felt lighter.

I snapped a few pictures of the moss-covered rocks that lined the path to a waterfall. I'd become pretty savvy with the camera settings for zooming and opted for a selfie with the waterfall behind me. I felt like Inspector Gadget with his Go-Go Gadget arms every time I used the 0.5× option, but I loved what I was able to capture by zooming out so much. Although I wished that Tye and Antonio were with me, I recognized that had they been there, I might not have connected with people like Emme, Grayce, and Geo.

I spotted a tree stump and stopped to change into my water shoes. I stepped over some exposed tree roots toward the stream and walked into the water. I gathered a few stones in varying sizes and decided to build a cairn. It took me some time to find the right stones to stack, but it ended up being time well spent. As I worked to balance all the stones in different sizes and shapes to build the cairn,

I discovered that some were too jagged, some were too muddy, and others were too heavy, causing the pile to fall. Was this a problem, or was it an opportunity to be creative in building the cairn? I captured some great pics of my first cairn build and felt an unusual sense of excitement to share them with my pastor. I remembered a sermon he delivered about being solutions-focused in life. Prior to this trip, I wouldn't have thought to take a picture of the cairn pile and share it with my pastor. I smiled.

I changed out of my water shoes, grabbed my hiking stick, and continued on the trail to an alcove, where I came across a plaque. I wondered if it was more about the moonstone.

The sign read:

> *This pristine, protected land marks the home for wildlife. Similar to those who are reading this, animals travel through the area every day, but few capture the attention like this visitor did. A lone wolf was spotted here for the first time in over a century. His yellow eyes are associated with embodying the spirit of the wild with determination and fearlessness in the face of challenges. The lone wolf can survive, but wolves thrive even better in packs. Hikers, we encourage you to travel our trails in packs.*

Whoa! I thought to myself. I wasn't sure what I would do if I saw a wolf. I would likely ring my bear bell but had no idea if that would be effective. I hoped I wouldn't have to test the bear bell on this trip.

Scrolling through my photos from this hike on my descent, I couldn't believe the unexpected series of experiences. From seeing Emme and learning about moonstone, to building a cairn, to reading about the wolf sighting, my wheels were turning.

I got to my truck and texted Emme the pic of the lone wolf sign: *Great to see you today! Thought you'd appreciate this message. As a wise woman once told me, I encourage you to share this pic with your mentor and thank her for the reminder to find your pack.* I added the wink emoji and packed up my truck.

I was half-listening to my classical playlist on the drive back to the cabin as I reflected on the day. I looked forward to connecting with Grayce to connect the dots. I wondered if anybody considered me part of their pack. When I got to the cabin, I opened my journal and made a new entry.

Be Brilliant

Friday 6:00 p.m.
I keep thinking about my connection to being a lone wolf. I always embraced that as a badge of honor – like, I don't need anyone or anything. I always considered my commitment to doing things myself as a sign of strength and independence. I am beginning to rethink that. Maybe having a pack is something I was afraid of given my resolute nature. I am not always a fan of other people's opinions. Nor do I need help. Or do I?

I can't get Emme's story about how her mentor helped her not to be a lone wolf off my mind. It's pretty wild that I even met Emme in the first place. The note her mentor gave her with the moonstone was such a powerful message, I will have to text her for the exact message, so I have it. I think it was something like the light of the moon can light the path forward in the dark. You need many moons in your life. Something like that. Are many moons the same as star clusters and pack members? I wonder. . . .

What were your Be Brilliant key learnings?

_____

_____

_____

_____

_____

_____

_____

CHAPTER
10

Proto*star*

I went to the lodge Friday night just before sunset and waited for Grayce to arrive for her Friday evening of stargazing so I could tell her about the day's hike. The conversations each night were having a profound effect on me, and the connections she was making between the stars and my hikes had me even more inspired and interested. The hike I had completed that day hurt so good – 10 miles of peace. I learned so many lessons during the hike, and I had been personally making threads of connections from my journal and each hike.

I spotted Geo standing alone in the grassy area by the lodge not too far from where Grayce always set up her telescopes. He had his duffle bag with him, and it looked like he was getting ready to leave. I walked over to say hi. He had beat me pretty badly at several games now, and we had formed a bit of a bond during the matches. Although our conversations were very surface level, we seemed to connect.

"Hi, Geo," I said.

"Hey," he replied.

"Are you getting ready to head home?"

Geo nodded.

"You look a bit down. You going to miss this place?" I asked.

Geo looked down at his shoes and softly said, "I'm okay."

"Are you sure?" I knew something was up.

Geo looked in my direction.

"In about two years I'll finish college. It will be a great accomplishment for me. I've overcome a lot of adversity in my life. Navigating my disability, getting an education, and becoming a successful chess player are all great, but I do not feel fulfilled. I feel like there is something I am supposed to be doing. I don't want to go work at my parents' business after college. I mean, I could and it would be a good job, but I need something that helps me find joy and inspires others. I feel like other people would benefit from hearing my story who are dealing with things of their own. That's what I want to do." As Geo said these things, I could hear the emotions well up in his voice.

We were pretty close to the core of learning and growth. I asked Geo to walk with me and took him into the center of the rope circle.

"Geo, we're standing at the proximal part of the park," I said.

"Proximal?" Geo inquired.

"Yes, this this the center. 'Proximal' means 'located near the center,' and this is the core of learning and growth."

I pointed to the clouds in the night sky and continued, "You see all those clouds up there? They're blocking us from seeing the entire sky, Geo, but in fact what is illuminated on clear nights tells an amazing story. Sometimes there may be clouds in your life that make the bigger picture unclear, but what we see depends on what lens we choose. Clouds may hide the stars, but only for a time. In life, as in the sky, the greatest beauty often lies in the ability to wait for the clouds to pass, revealing the brilliance that was always there. Just as clouds cover the sky but cannot dim the light of the stars, don't let those clouds detract from what truly can be revealed for you, Geo."

I put my hand on his shoulder.

Geo said, "But how will I know what will truly be revealed? I feel I have so much to offer. I just don't know how to start."

I smiled. "It's natural to find ourselves at crossroads, entangled in conflict, Geo. But remember, conflict is not just a barrier; it's a catalyst for clarity. Consider the stars. When two galaxies draw near each other, their gravity leads to the creation of new stars, a new birth as the result of tension. This new star formation shows us how conflicts can drive us to create new ideas and illuminate our path. This can be a lesson in resilience and creativity, akin to the energy of the butterfly jasper stone, which inspires us to embrace our imaginations and tackle challenges with courage. Embrace the conflict, Geo, because in the heart of turmoil is where new ideas, like new stars, are born."

Geo listened and nodded. "I have so many ideas, Jack. I want to spread them to the world, but I just don't know how!"

"I understand, and I feel that too, Geo. It's natural. On my last hike I realized that the lone wolf navigates the wilderness with unwavering determination on a journey of self-discovery and personal truth. Sometimes in the dark we need the light of the moon to illuminate the path forward. Do you know what the moonstone symbolizes?"

Geo shook his head no but wondered, "Does it bring us light?"

"Sort of. It encourages introspection and understanding of one's true path. It seems like you want to help others, Geo. It's just a matter of figuring out how. Your journey can be one of purpose and impact if you choose. It reminds me of the Beehive Cluster in the night sky, where tightly gathered stars in the constellation Cancer shine collectively brighter than they would alone. Just like that, your path and the work you decide to do can light up the darkness, bringing light to unclear ideas and making something beautiful. In your aspiration to help others, you're like a bee that pollinates flowers. Your role, much like the bee's, is essential in unveiling the beauty and potential in everything around us."

Geo chuckled. "Jack, how do you know so much about all this stuff? Are you some sort of geologist-astronomer-beekeeping savant?"

I laughed. "Not at all. I am no astronomer. I just. . ."

Before I could get the full thought out, a voice chimed in. "He most certainly is. He is actually an amateur stargazer, Geo."

It was Grayce. Apparently, she and Geo had already met.

"You're a stargazer, like Grayce?" Geo asked me.

"No, Geo, I'm not a stargazer."

But Grayce contradicted me. "On the contrary, Geo. He just hasn't figured out what that really means quite yet."

I looked at Grayce, confused. She nodded her head, smiled, and raised her brow, as if to say, *In time, my friend.*

"So this makes sense," Geo said. "Jack, will you become part of my star system?"

"Star system?" I questioned.

"Yes. You didn't learn about that one from Grayce?"

She said, "I have not yet revealed to Jack what I shared with you, Geo. Do you think I should share it with him?"

Geo nodded. "Definitely. I want Jack to be part of my star system, Grayce. So he needs to know what that is."

"Geo, I think Jack would be someone perfect for your star system," Grayce replied.

She turned to Jack. "Tonight is Friday, when I usually have my largest crowd for stargazing, so I may not be able to give the conversation the required time tonight. But I'd like to make sure we can both Be Present for the star system conversation. How about I swing by tomorrow morning before you head out?"

Before I could say yes, Geo chimed in. "Why don't you do a hike together?"

"How about it?" I asked Grayce. "I would love to hear about star systems."

"Sure, Jack. A hike sounds great."

"What do you say we meet at the visitors center at 8:00 a.m.? You can pick out a hike for us tonight. Just make it moderate for me, Jack, and I will see you tomorrow."

I looked at Geo, who was nodding and giving me a kind of wingman smirk. I gave him a glance and a smile.

Grayce began setting up her telescopes and I walked Geo to his dad, who was waiting patiently by the car.

"So, Geo, are you trying to play matchmaker?" I asked him.

He laughed. "I just thought it would be great for you to hear about star systems, Jack. Your advice really resonated with me, and I want us to stay connected."

We hugged and exchanged numbers. I told him I would be in touch, and he and his father drove off. I turned back and looked at where Grayce was. The park was filling up with the weekend crowd, and the BBQ area was packed. Grayce had a line of people. I wanted to tell her about my hike on White Wolf Trail, but I left her with her customers. I gave a wave, and she waved back and mouthed, "I'll see you tomorrow."

I went back to the cabin and sat on a stool at the kitchen countertop. I wanted to find the perfect hike for Grayce and me. I pulled open the app and began reading all the reviews and difficulties, seeking just the right

balance of challenge and enjoyment. After being immersed
in an hour of scrolling and reading reviews, I was worried
I would forget the great conversation with Geo, so I
opened my journal to write down my thoughts.

Be Brilliant

Friday 9:55 p.m.
Everyone here is so friendly. In my daily life, I interact
with people who come to my vineyard, but beyond that
I rarely seek out opportunities to talk to people. This
week has been very different. My interactions have
been so meaningful and thought-provoking, almost in a
scary way. I am beginning to wonder if I truly know
myself. I seem to have more questions than answers! I
am so happy I started this journal to prompt me to
reflect on the things from the day. It's been such an
energizing exercise.

I am thinking about Geo asking me to be in his star
system and then his reference to me as a stargazer.
It's nice of Grayce and Geo to toot my horn to be nice,
but they don't really know me. I've never really thought
about any of this before, so how the heck can I be a
stargazer? It seems that being a "Stargazer" means
making meaningful connections with how the stars align
to life.

What were your Be Brilliant key learnings?

_____

_____

_____

_____

_____

_____

_____

CHAPTER 11

Lode*star*

The next morning, Grayce met me at the visitors center, and we greeted each other with a hug. She had her hiking backpack on and a reusable water bottle, and she looked ready to tackle the day. I asked her if she wanted to grab a little breakfast, but she said she had already eaten.

The hike I had chosen was a moderate one, around six miles. The reviews of Impression Peak Vista Trail said there were beautiful vistas at the top of the peak, and you could see waterfalls that gave the impression they were falling from the sky and stopping when they hit the tops of trees. I thought that sounded so interesting and wanted to see it.

The trail was a short drive from the visitors center, so we chatted about all the people who had come by the previous night to stargaze.

"It was one of my busiest nights," Grayce told me. "Once the clouds moved out, so many celestial objects became visible. The best thing to see clearly is the moon, but people are curious about the stars and the constellations. You can see some planets, but most stars just look like small dots in the sky. Artificial intelligence and color-enhanced photos make these objects look so surreal on the NASA website, and most people are expecting them to look that way through an amateur telescope. So I help them understand the tools that we're using and what to look for. I explain to them what most astrophysicists and amateur astronomers recognize, which is that it's very difficult to see the actual beauty without the right environment and tools."

"You mean better telescopes and clear skies?" I asked.

"Well, not just clear skies, but really dark skies. When the light pollution is bad, it's often hard to see what's above us. You need the environment to be ideal, and as far as the tools go, without the proper telescopes and lenses, you cannot truly become curious."

"The stronger the telescope, the more you see," Jack said confidently.

"True," Grayce laughed. "But gazing upon the cosmos, we're reminded that the right environment can turn curiosity into a quest for knowledge and even transform it into innovation."

"That's so powerful, Grayce," I said, which prompted a smile in return.

We pulled up to the trailhead and parked. It was around 8:15 a.m. on Saturday and the trail looked like it was bustling. We got our gear and downloaded the map from the park app in case reception was bad, which was usually the case on the mountain. We took a selfie by the entrance to Impression Peak Vista Trail and started on our way.

The trail was made of hard-packed dirt with jagged stone, and it was easy to quickly become hidden in the canopy of trees. The incline started no more than 10 feet in, and the elevation climb had us breathing a little more heavily. The many trees meant that raised tree roots crisscrossed the trail, so we had to be cautious not to trip on the exposed roots. The path was wide enough for two people, but it was also an out-and-back trail, so we anticipated having to walk single file when other hikers were on their way back down.

We walked quietly for a bit, then I broke the silence. "You know, I was going to invite you on a hike even before Geo mentioned it."

"You were!" she said. "Well, I'm glad you both thought of it. I love hiking."

We were both leaning forward as the inclination became a little more intense.

"So you call this is a moderate hike, Jack?" she said, smiling but also panting.

"That's what the reviews said."

We walked for about an hour. I learned more about her background and her family, her passion for teaching, and her decision to do this amateur astronomy each night to better support herself financially. I acknowledged that teachers' pay was not where it should be, and we talked a bit about how to influence that.

She brought up a friend's wedding she had attended at a farm a couple years ago and how making a connection with someone there had changed her life. That was where she learned that she could choose who and how she wanted to be. She also discovered that helping pollinate and be a growth partner for others was something that had been missing in her life.

I listened to her and shared my story, too. We laughed and joked. It was great company.

When we got to the end of Impression Peak Vista Trail, Grayce and I just stared at the surreal views for a few minutes in silence. There was something to be said for quietly enjoying nature alone with your thoughts. We walked around a bit to look out on the horizon from different points. Various hikers were taking pictures, enjoying the view, eating snacks, and rehydrating on nearby rocks. The tip of the peak was as big as a cul-de-sac, and we learned that the reason it was called Impression Peak was not because it had a peak of its own, but because you could see a number of the surrounding mountain range's peaks in the distance.

"Jack," Grayce said. "Check this out." She motioned me over to a wooden sign next to a large stone, similar to the other signs I had often seen at the end of my hikes.

I took a moment to read the sign:

> *Impression jasper is a stone of tranquility and encouragement. This is a stone that unifies lives and reminds people to help one another. Impression jasper absorbs negative energy and aligns the body, mind, and spirit.*

"Another rock with yet another important message. Well, this trip has really made an impression on me, so this is very appropriate." We shared a laugh.

We sat on a rock at the vista and ate some nuts and an apple I had brought. I thought about how the connections we make between things we have recently seen or talked about is so important. Some people might dismiss that as recency bias, but I truly believed that everything happens for a reason.

Grayce said, "So I never actually heard about your hike at White Wolf Trail, Jack. I think I heard you mention something to Geo about the moonstone and being a lone wolf?"

"Actually, it's funny you ask, because I've been wondering whether anyone considers me to be part of their pack."

"What do you mean, Jack?"

"Emme told me about how her mentor encouraged her to find strength in her pack, and I realized that thinking in a pack mentality doesn't come naturally to me."

"I disagree, Jack. I think you don't allow yourself to be vulnerable enough to need others, but you could. That mentality is up to you. Let's keep unpacking this, Jack."

At the vista a sign announced, "Impression Peak Summit Trail – 1 mile," pointing up a rocky mountainous path. There were some warning signs saying not to go alone, to be careful, and that mild rock climbing and traversing were required. Some people were walking back down as we had been talking and we could tell that they were both excited and relieved.

We had a couple of choices. We could turn back and finish the last three miles of the six-mile moderate hike, or we could tackle the Impression Peak Summit Trail, which was an extra mile. I was not sure what Grayce wanted to do.

"You want to tackle Impression Peak Summit Trail?" I asked.

She nodded excitedly. "Let's do it. I love your sense of curiosity."

We began the hike to the summit of Impression Peak. The walk was ascending, and the trees were marked with blue paint to denote the trailhead. It was very rocky terrain, and a person had to be very careful not to lose their footing. I stopped for a minute and grabbed some sturdy walking sticks.

"I think I'm ready to hear about star systems," I said to Grayce. "Why didn't you tell me about them earlier? They seem important."

Grayce looked at me and smiled, as if acknowledging it might be time. "Jack, sometimes timing is everything. You know how you just told me about being a lone wolf? I already had some intuition that you were a lone wolf. Before someone can appreciate the importance of a star system, they must be ready. You need to have the right environment, the right time, and a strong willingness to accept help."

"How did you know Geo was ready and decide to tell him?" I asked.

"Geo is a chess player, Jack. A game where the interdependencies of many pieces are required to achieve a goal. Geo knows that about chess and he knows that about himself. It was clear to me Geo was willing to accept help, learn, and grow. Not everyone is as obvious," she said with a wink. "I heard you talking to Geo. What you told him was so profound. It was like you synthesized the learnings from your hikes and our conversations so beautifully and created so many threads of connections, and you. . ." Grayce's sentence trailed off, and she stopped walking and simply stared.

The path opened to a small clearing on the mountainside where people could study the surrounding mountains and take pictures. We spent a minute appreciating the view of the breathtaking red rocks and mountains. With all the talks about the universe and planets, these views sometimes gave me the impression that we weren't even on this world.

"I guess this is why they call it Impression Peak," I said. I motioned Grayce over and asked if she wanted to snap a selfie with me. She nodded and we had a moment trying to capture the best angle.

When we continued walking, she picked up the conversation on star systems.

"Where was I? Oh, right. Jack, I loved how you made all those connections for Geo. It was obvious to Geo you cared, listened, and had consistently made time with him to connect. You demonstrated real knowledge of the stars and the lessons from the hikes, and he must have seen that you have the commitment and competence to help him see the things that he may not yet be seeing. In the short time with Geo, you demonstrated the four 'C's, so trust was built."

I asked, "What are the four 'C's?"

"When people demonstrate care and communication, competence, consistency, and commitment, they are demonstrating the four 'C's and then people begin to trust you. This is the first piece in building a star system, or a pack, or an internal board of directors – whatever you want to call it, Jack. Identifying people in your circle, life, and network you trust who can help you be brighter, richer, and stronger together. Geo came to stargaze one night and shared with me what was on his mind. He was soul searching. He wanted to make an impact in the world but was struggling to put together the thoughts in his head. He was trying to go it alone, much like the lone wolf you mentioned. The lone wolf mentality can only get you so far, so you need to find a pack. That is when I pointed to one of the constellations in the sky, Orion specifically. I showed Geo that each one of those stars is bright, but together they are brighter and stronger. I told him to go on a journey and find the stars in his life he can assemble. A team of people he trusts who can act as a source of growth. I told Geo that the first step for him to uncover his true potential starts with him building a personal star system. A few days later he asked you to be one of the stars in his system. How many times did you interact with Geo on this trip?" Grayce asked.

"We played chess and talked a couple of times, and then our meeting last night where you saw me talking."

"It wasn't a meeting, Jack. It was a personal connection between you and Geo."

I recognized in that moment that I sometimes viewed interactions as meetings when I should have been thinking about them as connections. This was probably true to my personality and style and perhaps people felt this.

"As you think about building your own star system, Jack, you need to find those stars in your life you feel connected to and who are a source of growth for you. Your star system will help you choose who and how you want to be. They will help you learn to be proximal and they in return will demonstrate the art of learning to be proximal with you."

The art of learning to be proximal. That really resonated with me. I had written about being proximal in my journal several times this week.

Grayce continued, "Everything exists for a reason: the stars, the planets, the jasper stones you've seen, the landscape on this trail, and the people in your life. The skills and talents you were given can be maximized if you build your star system. Allow people to help and support you, and then you can become the source of growth for everyone who has asked you to be in their star system."

I nodded in agreement.

"And to top it off, Jack, we are collectively bigger than one person. Surrounding yourself with a personal constellation of talents, each star with its unique brilliance, forms the basis on which each of the individuals can flourish. This star system, carefully curated, enables each star within it to navigate life's challenges, leveraging diverse strengths and perspectives for personal growth."

"So each person within the star system gets stronger and thrives," I observed.

"Exactly. But it isn't just the individual stars. It's the whole constellation. When you finally have a star system that is aligned and you inspire others whom you work with and through with the intentional gravitational pull of a shared mission, it can form a very cohesive team. This synergy not only helps illuminate a team's collective strength, but also propels organizations toward uncharted territories and sustainable growth. While individual stars can guide us, the entire constellation together creates the most brilliant illumination. This is why you need to build a star system, Jack."

I thanked Grayce and acknowledged that this was some of the most valuable information she had shared with me. I asked her if we could stop for a moment so I could capture this in my journal while it was still fresh in my mind. We took a 10-minute break, and she sat down and drank some water. I took out my journal. While I was writing, I felt simply at peace.

Be Brilliant

Saturday 10:45 a.m.

What does it mean to be part of a star system? I wonder what criteria I should use for building my own star system. I am both frustrated and inspired that I have more questions than answers as I reflect on these experiences. I wonder if a star system can help me keep myself and others at the core of learning and growth. How will I do this for Geo?

I have always thought of myself as a trustworthy person. But is this the same thing as building trust? Who knew there were four "C"s to trust building? Consistency, care, commitment, and competence. It sounds simple on the surface, but I'm going to need to keep these in mind as I communicate with people.

What were your Be Brilliant key learnings?

_____

_____

_____

_____

_____

_____

_____

CHAPTER
12

Rockstar

Impression Peak's summit was close now, but we had to do a bit more climbing to reach it. In front of us horizontal ledge offered a climbing rope fixed to the side of the mountain to aid people in crossing. It looked to be only about 30 yards across, but I remembered that Grayce had originally told me she wanted to do just a moderate hike. This looked a little more intense than we'd expected.

"Grayce, it looks like we need to make another decision here. Do you want to keep going up, or would you rather head back down?"

"We're almost there now, Jack. I say we do it!"

A family of four appeared from the other direction, so we watched carefully as we waited for them to cross first. The mom was in front, the two teenage kids in the middle, and the dad brought up the rear. I wondered if I would have done the same if I were in his situation. I probably would have wanted to be in the middle, so I could help in the back and in the front. As they all finished crossing, I could hear the wife anxiously say, "You should have led the way instead of me. I almost slipped." So I figured no matter what I would have done in his shoes, it was potentially a no-win scenario.

"Ready?" Grayce asked as she grabbed onto the climbing rope first and started out.

I slowly followed. We shimmied across the mountain with ease, focused only on taking each next step and ensuring we did not step off the ledge and slide down the mountain. I looked down and was a little reassured when I realized that the flat area not far below meant that someone would easily survive the slip, but I was certainly being cautious anyway.

A few minutes after we crossed the roped ledge, we reached the summit. The air was crisp and clear, a stark contrast to the exertion that had brought us up the mountain to this point. As we stood on the summit, a profound sense of peace came over us. The challenges of the climb and traversing this mountain seemed insignificant compared to the beauty that lay before us.

This moment atop Impression Peak was a reminder of the rewards that await those who dare to take difficult paths. It was a testimony to the resilience of the human spirit, a symbol of what you can achieve not just in overcoming a challenge, but in moving forward through anxiety.

"This view," Grayce said.

We were both in awe. The view was not just a physical landscape. It was metaphorical for the possibilities that open when one perseveres through life's challenges.

"Jack, how does it feel?" Grayce asked.

"I feel like I was immersed in making sure that neither of us fell."

"Jack, this is why you need to build your star system."

"What do you mean?"

"We just traversed a rock face, where you said you were fully focused, just like every grasp and step in life represent a challenge demanding focus, skill, and resilience. This is the journey of achieving flow, Jack, a state of immersive engagement and peak performance. Think of the people in your personal star system as your fellow climbers. They secure your ropes, ensuring safety and support, allowing you to take risks and push boundaries. They're the ones who spot the best paths, share techniques, and encourage you when the ascent seems insurmountable.

Each person contributes uniquely to your climb, much like different grips and ledges on the rock face. Some offer the sturdy support needed for rest and reassessment, like a wide ledge. Others challenge you to stretch further, reach higher, and embrace the thrill of the climb, like a demanding narrow ledge that tests your limits."

Grace paused for a moment and then continued. "Achieving flow is like finding a path that balances challenges with skill, demanding your full attention and best efforts, yet feels rewarding and exhilarating. The people in your star system help you maintain this balance, enabling you to achieve and sustain flow, both individually and as a team. Together, you not only conquer any challenges but also optimize performance, transforming daunting tasks into reaching your summit. This can only be created with what we talked about earlier – trust and shared purpose. It just goes to show how collective support from your star system and individual effort align to elevate performance to its peak, in the pursuit of shared goals and personal growth."

That was such an amazing analogy. We had spent three hours on this mountain, and I could not believe all that I had learned – proof that so much growth can happen in such a short period of time.

"I feel like you're a natural at this, Grayce. So profound."

"I put myself at the center of people's growth. I learned this from someone in my star system. Her name is Catherine. She helped me decide who and how I wanted to be, and if it not for her, I'm not sure we'd be here today."

We began to make our way back down the mountain. The time passed much more quickly on the descent. After our journey to the summit, we had more confidence about the trail. We kept looking at pictures we had taken, despite the downhill rocky terrain. When we got to the trailhead at the end, we took one last photo. It was around 2:00 in the afternoon, and we were both famished.

Before we hopped into my truck, I said, "I consider you to be my personal growth rockstar. I learned so much from you, Grayce. If I knew what a star system was before this, I'm sure I would ask you to be in mine."

"Well, Jack, if this is an invitation to stay connected and become a member of your star system, I must say there might have been a more meaningful way to ask."

While I appreciated her subtle nod to my lack of awareness with that comment, true to my style, I paused. "Grayce, will you be the first person in my star system? I already feel I am a brighter, richer, and stronger human being because of you."

"Of course, Jack. It would be my honor. You have made such beautiful connections between the stars and stones, and I would love to help you on whatever personal journey you go on."

Stars and stones, I thought to myself. That had such a nice ring to it.

I thanked her and drove us back to the visitors center. Grayce and I exchanged contact information, and I told her I'd keep in touch. We gave each other a warm embrace that lasted a while.

When I got back to my cabin to grab my bags to leave, I took out my journal and added to what I had already written.

Be Brilliant

Saturday 4:05 p.m.

I can't believe this experience. I remember a college professor mentioned the idea of experiencing an epistemological crisis in the learning process. I was experiencing this after the last few days; I don't know what I know or why I know what I know or don't know. But I do know that I am not ready to go home. I also know that I have a lot to learn and unlearn. I just flipped back a few pages to Grayce's advice that I wrote about on Tuesday night. She reminded me, "You can't learn anything new until you are open enough to forget everything you think you know." Am I open? What do I know?

This leads me to think of what Grayce shared with me about the experience of flow. I love the idea of being in a state of immersive engagement and peak performance. Grayce mentioned that the people in your star system help you maintain a balance of challenge and skill, enabling you to achieve and sustain flow, both individually and as a team. But this all relies on relationships grounded in trust. The process of building a star system seems so complicated. Is it worth the energy?

As I look at my journal, I can see so many lessons that I have learned from Grayce. But they're just a glimpse of our conversations. And she knows so much more that we haven't even discussed. Maybe I need to follow up with Grayce on several things. I can't believe I'm writing this, but I'm feeling a little emotional. I am going to miss her. . . .

What were your Be Brilliant key learnings?

_____

_____

_____

_____

_____

_____

_____

CHAPTER
13

*Star*bright

I was so happy I'd stayed at the park, despite being sad that my friends Antonio and Tye could not make it. But I felt like we were connected because of our text exchanges and their genuine curiosity about what I was doing. I think they were jealous.

Before I left the park, I stopped by the souvenir shop in the visitors center. The shop had all sorts of stuff – animals, books, the gemstones from each hike, compasses, maps, and so many other goodies. I flicked open a small gold compass and moved it around. It reminded me of my first night where the telescopes were pointing in four different directions.

I walked over to the gemstones and as I sifted through them like a kid, my head played back some of my aha moments. I needed to make sure I kept this feeling after the trip. As I moved my fingers through the smooth, colorful stones, I noticed that some of them were the stones I had read about on my hikes. They had butterfly, bumblebee, starburst, and impression jaspers, and moonstones. Looking at the small burlap bags that were designed to hold the stones gave me a brilliant idea! Coming off the heels of my star system conversation, I wanted to make sure I had something to give to each person I asked to be in my star system. I made five bags, with all the stones from my hikes and a compass in each one.

When I left the visitors center, I took one last walk over to the rope circle, which had become known as the core of learning and growth, and saw Vincent, the park ranger.

"You heading out?" he asked.

"Yes, unfortunately. Have to get back to reality."

"Happy you stayed, I take it?" he smiled.

"Yes, thank you for the encouragement. It was just what I needed. Can I ask you a favor, Vincent?"

"Sure, tell me," he said.

I pulled out one of the little bags of stones with the small compass and handed it to him.

"Can you give this to Grayce when you see her?"

"Ah, a little gift! You bet. I will give this to her next time I see her." He put the bag into his khaki cargo pants pocket.

"Thanks, Vincent."

We shook hands and said goodbye.

The drive home was peaceful as I reflected on all my experiences. I knew the first thing I needed to do was build my star system. I had already asked Grayce and she was in, for which I was so appreciative. She had helped illuminate for me what it means to be at the core of learning and growth. I needed to recognize the people in my life who could help me see the things I did not, challenge me, and help me move away from the lone wolf mentality so I could grow.

My vineyard had so many opportunities for growth. I now realized the reason it had not been going as planned was because I was not letting people support me. I could think of the people in my life who shone brightly. There were stars in my life who had supported me and been there for me. Tye, Antonio, and Uncle Mike were all names that popped into my head. I came to the realization that Geo was someone who should also be in there. Even though we had just met, we had formed a bond and a connection. He had moved me out of my comfort zone to do things that I otherwise might not have done for a while. I needed people like this encouraging me.

When I arrived home early Saturday evening, I partially unpacked and went to bed. I was exhausted. I must have logged over 40 miles of hikes.

Sunday morning, I went to church and was just grateful. I took the rest of the day to collect my thoughts, decompress, recharge, and walk the vineyard. The grapes were growing beautifully, and before we knew it, August would arrive for harvest. I sat outside the main building and poured myself a cup of pomegranate tea with manuka honey. My vineyard spread up the hillside in the distance. Just beyond it, my property extended into the low mountains that were part of the Yountville Hills. I'd walked them many times, including a rocky part that I sometimes climbed. It made me think of my conversation with Grayce about flow and the focus needed. Sipping my tea, I pulled out my journal, reviewed what I'd written, and reflected on my journey. I didn't want my journey to stop now that I was back home. I wanted to achieve the flow that I'd discussed with Grayce. I decided to do something completely out of the norm for me, something I found unbelievably nerve-wracking. I went onto social media and posted a video.

"Hi, everyone! I just returned from an unexpectedly soul-nourishing week of hiking. While out in nature, I learned so much about the power of stars and the stones. Earth stones provide us with health benefits, and stars work together in constellations to shine more brightly. We can use what they teach us to improve our minds and bodies and to drive well-being and growth."

My vineyard's Instagram account had a little over a hundred followers. The positive comments came pouring in, and I saw that some of the followers started sharing the post with others.

The next day I posted another video.

"Quick tour of the vineyard, everyone. I'm standing at the center, and I'm going to draw this circle with my heel right in the center. The next time you see this spot, it will be the core of learning and growth."

Again, the comments came in. Some people asked, "What is the core of learning and growth?" One person said, "Nice beard, dude." But the followers grew.

I started doing more videos and social media posts to try to bring to life the insights from my journal.

I decided it was time to invite people to my star system, and I reached out to my list.

Uncle Mike

I called my uncle to see if we could meet up. I knew he'd had a tough year and was getting older, but if I was going to begin to build my own personal star system like Grayce had taught me about, my uncle had to be in it.

We met up that afternoon and talked for hours. I told him about my trip and shared my experiences from the journal. I could sense he appreciated this moment and my companionship. I felt the same way. After he sold the vineyard to me, I'd been so busy that we just hadn't had as much time together as we used to.

I shared with him my vision to turn the vineyard into more than just a place where people learned about and tasted wine. I wanted to bring people here on retreats to connect the earth, mind, and body. There were so many lessons I learned from the stars and stones, and our vineyard could be the perfect place to create a new narrative. Most people come to the vineyard to taste wine, but maybe we could attract groups to come and learn even more together.

I explained the principles I was thinking about teaching to help teams and people become brighter, richer, and stronger together that I had mapped out in my journal. We could connect the lessons to the same principles we used as vintners, which included:

- The right environment
- Watering and pruning our vines to achieve optimal growth
- Timing of the harvest
- Trusting the process of making wine

The process we went through was not too dissimilar from building high-performing teams and organizations.

I could sense a renewed focus from Uncle Mike. I think he liked where I was going with this. I told him there was going to be a lot of work to do, but rebranding and thinking differently would be the catalyst for our growth. I told him how I learned about building my star system and that I wanted him to be someone in that star system. I asked if we could be growth partners and help bring the vision to life.

We got up and hugged. The second member of my star system was born – Uncle Mike.

The energy from my conversation with Uncle Mike did not dissipate. I knew exactly what I needed to do!

Geo

It was around 6 p.m., and I texted Geo: *Hi Geo, it's Jack. How's it going? Do you want to play chess?*

I received an invite almost instantaneously from Geo from a chess app, which I had to download.

Hi Jack! I just sent you a game request. We can start a game. But we don't need to rush to finish it all at once. We can play over time.

Sounds great, I texted back. *I wanted to get back to you about being in your star system. Grayce explained what that means and I would be honored to be in yours.*

AWESOME! Geo replied. *I would love that. I'm going to need all the help I can get as I figure out what to do after college.*

Well, let's keep playing chess and staying connected. I am here to help! But I have something else to ask, Geo.

Sure! Hit me.

Will you be a member of my star system too?

Me? he replied.

Yes you! You brought me back to chess, something I loved to do. And you helped me connect all the dots from my trip in such a meaningful way. I want us to remain close and support each other.

Geo replied, *I'd be proud for us to be stars in each other's star systems. Don't forget to turn on the chess app notifications so you don't miss a move. And make sure you have a chess set so we can play in person if I come by to see you some time.*

I texted back, *LOL! Sure thing.*

Geo was the third person in my star system. Despite my lone wolf leanings, personal connection had always been important to me. We had developed mutual respect after a short amount of time. I knew that he had dreams of helping others, and he was the one who got me interested in chess again. I'd forgotten how much happiness and joy it had brought me, and picking it up again renewed my spirit. All too often people focus on tasks and trivial things in their personal and work lives and forget the simple things that bring impact.

I went online and bought a small chess set. I also got one of those giant chess sets that can be used outside, with pieces two to three feet tall; I would use this on the retreat. Grayce's comment about the interdependencies of these pieces and achieving a goal was a great lesson. By this time she was probably already setting up her telescopes at the core of learning and growth, so I resolved to call her the next day.

Grayce

I called Grayce in the late afternoon to catch her after teaching at the school but before she drove to the park. She said Vincent had given her my gift of the stones and compass, and she thought it was a wonderful way to ask people to be in my star system.

I shared that I had asked my Uncle Mike and Geo to part of my star system and reconfirmed she would be part of it too. I told her what I was thinking about setting up a corporate retreat at the winery and asked her for some ideas on how I could incorporate stargazing. She loved the idea and suggested some telescopes and some apps to explore to help with the stargazing process. We mapped out a plan on how to thread some lessons from the stars into the corporate training as it related to building a star system. She said she would love to help in any way possible. I viewed her as such a great resource and I almost told her that on the phone, but then I imagined her reaction to me calling her something as coldly clinical as a resource, so instead I thanked her for supporting me. We said goodbye and I wished her a great night of stargazing.

Grayce, Uncle Mike, and Geo were the first members of my star system. So many people in my life had helped me navigate challenges and grow and had been connected to me in meaningful ways. I was sure my star system would grow to shine even brighter, but for now this is who was helping me illuminate a path forward.

Antonio and Tye

I knew my friends wanted me to debrief them on the trip, so I scheduled time for a video call with them. When I thought about a star system, having good friends I could rely on and connect with in a meaningful way was critical. Over the years Antonio and Tye had been these people for me. They had helped me navigate life's difficulties but were also there as I celebrated milestones. They had provided a consistent ray of light and genuine care and concern. I recognized that memories were a big part of how my star system could shine brightly. Going through challenging situations together, reflecting on the good times and the bad, laughing and being a bit self-deprecating were all things that made me want them in my star system.

During our call I shared with them more details about the trip, my key learnings, and what I was thinking about for the vineyard. They showed their continued support and said they would certainly be members of what I now called my star system. On the screen, I showed them the bag of stones and the compass. I talked about how these stones became a source of encouragement and helped establish a mind-body connection. I told them I would be sending them each a bag as a gesture of gratitude for their support over the years. They said that I should consider changing the name of my vineyard and rebranding it. I thought this was a great idea.

CHAPTER
14

Stars and Stones

The next morning, I opened my journal and reread all the Be Brilliant lessons and learnings.

Based on my conversation with Antonio and Tye, I decided to change the name of my vineyard. My journal was my guide, and I had the perfect name. The lessons I reread helped me get inspiration from the stars and the stones. My vineyard would now be called "Stars and Stones," representing a nod to the stars and my star system and the inspiration from the stones.

Based on my conversations with my star system, I began to mentally map out on my computer what people would experience on the corporate retreat. I couldn't wait to bring these lessons to life in a meaningful way. There were seven lessons that immediately came to mind.

Choose Your Be Mindsets

I placed a circle at the center of the vineyard for the core of learning and growth. I wanted to establish the concept of Being Proximal and placing yourself at the core of your personal growth and others' growth as well. I believed there were significant teachable moments there for people visiting this corporate retreat. This is where people would choose who and how they wanted to be.

This place would be called "**Choose Your Be Mindsets**." This circular area would serve as the heart of the experience, symbolizing the vineyard's focus on personal development and enlightenment.

Open Eyes, Mind, Ears, and Heart

Based on my enthusiasm for chess and the connection to Geo, I wanted to use the large chess set that I had ordered to help people come to the retreat and understand the interdependencies of how the pieces work together. While I knew everyone might not like chess or even know how to play it, having a spot to sit and discuss this concept would be paramount.

This is the place where people would learn to **Open Eyes, Mind, Ears, and Heart**. Located to the northwest, just outside the core of learning and growth, this area would emphasize teamwork and strategic thinking. Its proximity to the central area would signify the importance of collaboration in personal growth.

Meaningful Work

The butterfly nebula and the connection to chaos theory was so inspiring. It showed how people create ripples and those small ripples can make bigger ripples in their lives. How do people reframe negative events to see positive opportunities? People can examine moments in their lives that seem trivial and see them as building blocks to something bigger. Understanding their purpose is essential.

The ability to understand **Meaningful Work** would be a critical component to the retreat. Positioned to the west of the core of learning and growth, this butterfly garden would be a place of beauty and transformation, reflecting the journey of growth and change. It would focus on things like chaos theory and the butterfly effect. It would provide a serene, natural element to the vineyard, inviting visitors to reflect.

Platinum Rule

We could build on this exercise by doing some trust training. There was a great spot on the vineyard where we had a small barn that used to be used for storage, but we could use it for horses. We build trust with horses when we show them that we are committed to consistently and competently caring for them, and we can build trust with people the same way.

This would be the perfect spot to incorporate the **Platinum Rule**. Situated to the southwest of the core of learning and growth, this area offered a focus on trust and working with horses to build trust. Treating others as they want to be treated is foundational to trust and demonstrates the four "C"s of competence, commitment, consistency, and care.

Always Be Proximal

Having people at the vineyard would be the perfect opportunity to demonstrate how teams could leverage fundamental wine-making concepts to optimize their performance. For example, ensuring that the environment is right and that you are always pruning and watering the vines is similar to ongoing development and nurturing of human beings. There is a very specific process to wine making, and understanding the importance of harvesting the grapes at the right time and trusting the process could be a great connection to what is required to build trust.

As a vintner you are responsible for placing yourself at the core of learning and growth. The **Always Be Proximal** area located slightly south of the core of learning and growth would be the perfect place to provide an appreciation of how the following items are required to make wine and are also needed for personal and professional growth.

- The right environment
- Watering and pruning our vines
- Timing of the harvest
- Trusting the process of making wine

Solutions-Focused Lens

One of the most impactful moments for me had been going on the hike with Grayce and traversing the rock wall. The conversation on flow and how we should challenge ourselves more to encourage the healthy form of stress had been really inspiring. At the retreat, I wanted an area for people to get out of their comfort zone and challenge themselves. This would be the time to convey how challenges help us grow by acquiring new skills and the knowledge to meet those challenges.

Situated to the east of the core of learning and growth, this **Solutions-Focused Lens** area would offer a physical challenge, emphasizing focus and flow. It would be a metaphor for overcoming obstacles through concentration and perseverance.

Shine Brighter and Stronger Together

Of course, we would need a spot for stargazing, where we could illuminate that the lens we choose can impact ourselves and others. This would be the spot for teams to understand how we are brighter, richer, and stronger together.

Placed north of the core of learning and growth, the area would encourage visitors to look beyond themselves, fostering a sense of wonder and curiosity about the universe. This would help participants learn how they could **Shine Brighter and Stronger Together**.

Finding the COMPASS

I literally shouted out loud! I loved it. I wanted to share this with my star system and let them know. I emailed them all my plan. These were separate emails, but each with the same message:

Thanks for your inspiration, conversations, and support of my vision to build the Stars and Stones retreat. I wanted to share with you my rough draft of what I put together. Is this the kind of thing you would want to visit?

Uncle Mike responded first:

This looks amazing. I love how you tied in the lessons from your trip. Looks like this is heading in the right DIRECTION.

Tye responded a few hours later:

Looks good to me! Happy to be the first one to test out the retreat! Can't wait to come out there. I won't have any problems finding you. lol

Later that evening, I got a text from Geo:

Saw your email. Sounds like you are too busy to play chess, but I like the fact that you have a framework. It's your move, by the way! Hey, looks like this thing can go in any direction, just like the queen.

The next morning I received an email from Antonio:

It looks like you found your true north. I love this concept. Let me know what you need.

The rest of the day I tended to the vineyard. Around 5:00 p.m. the phone rang, and it was Grayce.

"I've been meaning to call you and thank you personally for the stones and compass. I know I texted, but really it means a lot."

"My pleasure. It was the least I could do!"

We discussed her classes and how busy the stargazing had been. Then she said, "Hey, I loved your email by the

way! How did you come up with that? Was this all part of
your master plan?"

"I just used my notes and wrote down some activities
I think could help unleash the brilliance of building
brighter teams," I explained. "It was all from the learnings
on my hike, conversations with you, and discussions with
my star system."

"I understand that, silly. I meant the COMPASS
analogy. Did you give me a compass knowing ahead of
time that it was the plan?"

I laughed. "I have no clue what you're talking
about Grayce."

"The retreat. Using your compass to unleash the
brilliance of brighter teams. Your retreat lessons. . .they
spell COMPASS, right?"

I opened the plan that I'd sent to my star system. It did
spell compass:

- **C**hoose Your Be Mindsets
- **O**pen Eyes, Mind, Ears, and Heart
- **M**eaningful Work
- **P**latinum Rule
- **A**lways Be Proximal
- **S**olutions-Focused Lens
- **S**hine Brighter and Stronger Together

I'd had no clue. It was like the vision came to life in
such unsuspecting ways. "No, that's simply the stars
aligning," I told her. "I didn't plan it."

"Well, I love it, and I can't wait to be part of the growth
of Stars and Stones."

We said goodbye and I hung up. I realized the other people in my star system saw that this spelled COMPASS too. Their emails had all referenced the compass when they said "DIRECTION," "true north," "I won't have any problems finding you," and "go in any direction, just like the queen." I was curious how they had all noticed it, but I didn't really need to ask. It made me realize that this was a big part of choosing who and how I would be moving forward. Being curious was so important. It was a mindset I needed to embrace.

I reflected on how amazing it is that other people can sometimes see things that you can't. The people in your star system can illuminate things you may not see, and a deep connection between the people in your star system is paramount to personal and professional growth. The COMPASS framework would guide teams to unleash their potential, to shine brighter together, and to be more brilliant. Even if you can't always choose who and how you want to be on your own, the group of people around you can enable you to shine brighter.

I wanted to announce my plans to the world. I shot a quick video at the center of the vineyard and shared a message with everyone:

> "Here is how you can unleash the power of brighter and more brilliant teams! For more details on putting these ideas into action, follow Stars and Stones."

I tagged those who has Instagram accounts in my star system and used hashtags so people can find me including #starsystem and #bemindsets, to name a few. I shared the image of the COMPASS framework.

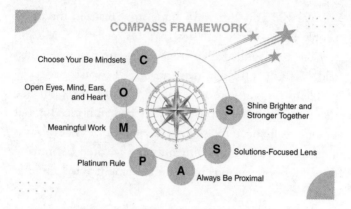

The responses were a bit overwhelming, with hundreds of likes, and my followership grew. I posted a video every day built around the COMPASS framework. I wanted to encourage a sense of community. The mind, body, and heart connection was real and the inspiration from the stones and the connection to my stars allowed for a newfound appreciation of how even a small vineyard could make a big impact. It seemed like my 11:11 wish from my first day's hike was coming true!

A Leadership Guide to Unleashing the Brilliance of Building Brighter Teams

Are you curious about what happened at Jack's "Stars and Stones" corporate retreat and why it became so popular? Are you wondering what Jack was going to do with all his newfound knowledge about stars and stones and how he was going to take the lessons from his trip and help others transform? Imagine hearing firsthand how he used his star system as a guiding light and how he brought his journal ideas to life.

Well, you're in luck! You get a chance to turn the telescope toward the first team to attend the corporate retreat. You'll experience how Jack applied his learnings to help individuals, teams, and organizations. Just as you can change the telescope's lens to see the stars more clearly and differently, you can do the same by changing the lens you use to look at life. How you see diversity of thought and voice, and how you receive key learnings, are paramount to your growth and development journey and are how you, too, can shape organizational culture. It all begins with the COMPASS. Using the COMPASS as a guide, you can unleash the power of building a brighter and more brilliant team.

Let's go behind the scenes and see what the members of this team experienced and how the learnings from the corporate retreat can help shape them.

The Stars and Stones Retreat Experience

An SUV carrying a small team of people rolled into the winery to experience the Stars and Stones retreat. In the SUV were Brad, Lillian, Kelly, Giules, Cole, and Maggie.

As the team emerged from the vehicle, they were greeted with a small glass of Zinfandel from the staff.

"Welcome to Stars and Stones," a jovial voice said. "I'm Mike, and I'll be your guide for the retreat."

Mike handed each member of the group a small burlap bag with a metal rock-climbing clamp attached to it. The bag sported the "Stars and Stones" logo stamped on the outside, and inside were some stones, a compass, and a small yellow and black bee charm.

"In this bag, you'll find some of the key ingredients to shining more brightly as a team. The purpose of this retreat is to illuminate the ways we can build more brilliant teams, and we're going to start with some self-reflection. Follow me."

Leadership Experience #1: Choose Your Be Mindset

Everyone followed Mike as he walked toward a large rope circle. "This circle here is the proximal part of the vineyard, meaning closest to the center. We call this first place the core of learning and growth. When people show up at this circle, they're ready to grow themselves, but more importantly to help their teams grow as well."

Once Mike had the team gathered around the rope circle, he continued. "Okay, group, first we need to come up with a team name, but I don't mean the name of the organization you come from. I want you all to take three minutes to align on what this team will be called here today."

The group started shouting out different names. There was a method to the madness of this exercise. Mike was observing the interactions of the team and watching their styles. He was making mental notes about how they interacted.

"Okay, your three minutes are up. What will be your team name?"

Lillian spoke up. "We decided on Team Wolfpack."

"And tell me how you decided on that," said Mike.

Lillian explained, "It's a nod to the strength of our pack!"

"Well, Team Wolfpack, since we're standing here at the core of learning and growth, it's time to ground ourselves and get ready to grow. I want you all to take a moment to look around."

The group paused and looked around.

Mike pointed to a small mountain in the distance. "Now I want you to look out upon that hill, where the mountains are. Now close your eyes and take a deep breath. Think about what mindset you're showing up with today. The first thing we need to do as a team is to choose our own personal mindsets. Your mindset of choosing who and how you will be is essential to fueling your team's growth. A more brilliant team starts with each of you individually."

Mike continued, "I want each of you to reach into your bags and pull out the compass and the bee. This small bee is representative of choosing who and how you will be, and your internal compass will be your guide on this retreat and as a team. Let the compass guide you to brilliance today."

Mike watched as they each found their compass and the yellow and black bee charm. They were all looking down, moving their compasses around to see the different directions.

"Now think about how you're showing up. Once you think of your Be mindset, step into the circle and share with your team," Mike said.

At first everyone was visibly uncomfortable, but after about five minutes of personal reflection and playing with the bee charm, the group started sharing their personal Be mindsets.

When they finished, Mike acknowledged each mindset. Then he challenged them to take some time to think of a team mindset that would drive them to be more brilliant together. The group started discussing a mindset that they would all want to be together. It was obvious that the team had been inspired by their previous uncomfortableness with the individual exercise because they were sharing a lot of ideas. The team chose the team mindset of "Be Bold." Maggie walked into the center of the circle and declared this team would be more brilliant if they embraced the "Be Bold" mindset.

Mike handed each member of the team a laminated Stars and Stones index card. He told them to hook this first card to the metal hook on the bag through the small hole in the top and take a moment to read their first leadership lesson.

Leadership Lesson for Teams

When teams are working to be more brilliant, it is easy to forget that each person on that team has a specific natural tendency or mindset, something that is important to them and drives them. As a leader, understanding how people show up and choose to Be is essential to the collective brilliance of the group. This exercise at a team meeting is to have individuals choose their own Be mindset but then collectively work to align on a team mindset that sets the tone for the team.

1. *Let people choose how they want to be and acknowledge their mindset. Ask them how this mindset fuels them.*

2. *Create a shared Be mindset as a team.*

3. *Put the individual Be mindsets on a slide that can be shared at every meeting, reminding the group how these mindsets play a role in optimizing the performance of each person, the team, and the organization.*

Note: This exercise can be replicated to kick off every subsequent New Year to encourage awareness and agency over each team member's choices.

Leadership Experience #2: Open Eyes, Mind, Ears, and Heart

The team was talkative after the first experience. Mike pulled the group back together.

"Everyone, listen up, I'd like you to reach in your bag and find this stone," he said as he held up the impression jasper. "This is a stone that unifies lives and reminds people to help one another. Impression jasper absorbs negative energy and aligns the body, mind, and spirit."

There was some chatter about the connection to the stone as the group followed Mike through the vineyard to a grassy area, where there were some tables with chessboards, and a very large chessboard with big chess pieces.

"Who knows anything about chess?" Mike asked.

Most of the team raised their hands.

"Who has played the game and knows what all the pieces do?"

About half the group raised their hands for that one.

"This chessboard is located very close to the center of the vineyard because the lesson you will learn here is paramount to the core of learning and growth. When we think of chess, it is all about strategy, teamwork, and how the many different pieces contribute to the execution of the strategy. When Jack, the owner, decided to add a chessboard to the retreat, it was not so people could learn how to play chess, although if you want to indulge in a game at lunch feel free," he chuckled. "It was so people could learn more about building brighter teams and how each different piece on a chessboard has a unique role and responsibility. They are collaborating, using each other's strengths to ensure that performance optimization at the individual level, team level, and organizational level is maximized."

Mike continued, "During this experience, we are going to focus on opening our eyes, mind, ears, and hearts. We are going to listen to understand and create a safe space for vulnerable and authentic conversations. Now I want you to each step into the large chessboard and stand next to a piece."

Everyone walked over and found a piece to stand next to. Even though there appeared to be a hierarchy in the team, people were reluctant to stand next to the biggest, most important pieces – the king and queen.

When everyone was in place, Mike spoke up. "Why did no one choose the king or queen?"

Cole spoke up: "I didn't want people to feel a certain way about my selections or that I was trying to assert control."

The same feedback was heard from the rest of the group.

"Interesting to hear this. It seems you all are trying to balance some humility," Mike said. "As we think about this chessboard, I want you to each take a turn and share why you think someone on your team should take the spot of the queen, which is the most dynamic, important, and versatile piece on the board. Tell me one another's strengths and why you think that person should have chosen the queen and how their strength can build a brighter team."

Each team member took turns choosing a queen, and multiple strengths were shared. People heard new things about themselves that their teammates had never told them before. Some genuine authentic moments were being shared.

Mike chimed in, "How did that feel?"

Everyone exclaimed how much they appreciated hearing this from the others, and how they wished they had done this exercise before as a team.

Mike handed each team member a laminated card that was checkered like a chessboard, with the image of the chess queen. On the back was a new leadership lesson.

Leadership Lesson for Teams

How can you encourage your team to be more open and encourage brilliance? Having people show up and encourage the utilization of strengths on the team is an essential leadership skill. It is equally important to understand the opportunities for growth. When we open our hearts and minds to let people put their skills to use, it becomes a catalyst for a brilliant team.

1. *Create a safe environment for people to open their eyes, mind, ears, and heart.*

2. *Have the team write down some of the strengths of the other people in the room and share them. Encourage everyone to write something down about everyone else. The more strengths, the better. This is the power of the Pygmalion Effect and a reminder that positive emotional contagion can fuel people.*

3. *Tell the team to remember the strengths they heard and ensure they are helping deploy those strengths at the individual, team, and organizational level.*

"Okay, Team Wolfpack! Follow me to the next experience. Bring your strengths, bring your mindsets, and especially bring your work ethic because we are going from doing only mental work to doing both mental and physical work."

Mike led the team down a winding trail through some trees that soon opened to a garden full of beautiful blooming flowers. There were some large white boxes in the distance that looked like beehives.

Leadership Experience #3: Meaningful Work

"Welcome to the butterfly garden at Stars and Stones." The group was meandering into the garden as Mike spoke.

"Time to reach in your burlap bags again, team." Mike held up a beautiful stone. "This one is called butterfly jasper. Fitting for where we're standing, right? This stone is said to enable a feeling of being free and help imagination soar to new heights. Butterfly jasper allows you to navigate transformation through any challenges life throws your way. It is said to clear the air while helping you stay true to your purpose and who you are as a person. Keep this stone in mind during your next experience."

Mike gestured toward the garden and said, "Take a walk around and enjoy the garden for a moment. I'll be right back."

As the team walked around and enjoyed the flowers, Mike brought out a number of small plants and some spades and gloves. He had some watering cans and some potting soil. He led them to an open area in the garden with a bench.

"Okay, Team Wolfpack! So far we explored our personal and team mindsets and shared our strengths with each other. I don't need to make a metaphor to the butterfly, because all of you know that butterflies are all about transformation. They need fuel to make the transformation and these plants here are the fuel. So we're going to give you each a plant, and your job is to expand the garden. Create more places for growth so we can create more butterflies. Come grab your plants and tools."

The team walked over and each person grabbed gloves, a spade, and some soil. The label on the plants said, "Milkweed."

The team members started walking around looking for the perfect spot. As Mike watched, he could see Brad bring the team together. They were conversing about something. The team all planted their milkweed in the same spot, together, and not around the garden in different areas. When the team was finished, they all gathered by the bench and grabbed some water. It was not a strenuous exercise, but it was nonetheless physical.

"Tell me, team, how did you enjoy the planting?" Mike asked.

Brad said, "When you asked us to grab the plants, I saw the team looking for their own spots, but I thought that we could plant all together and have our team be in one spot of the garden."

Mike smiled. "What a great way to help a team shine brighter and more brilliantly by doing things together. We should all try to find ways to create meaningful work for one another and ensure that we find meaning in our work at the individual, team, and organizational level. The keys to meaningful work are understanding these concepts:

- What is this team passionate about, and what are you passionate about as individuals?
- What does the team need to support the overall goals of the business?
- What is this team good at collectively?

"If we are not encouraging these behaviors to create meaningful work together, then there could be a ripple effect that has negative consequences. Ironically, one small ripple on the team that discourages meaning can lead to bigger ripples, which is called the butterfly effect."

Mike pulled out what seemed to be a carboard rectangle with a picture of a butterfly on it and a small hole pierced in one corner. He said, "This is made from seeds and recycled material. It's a reminder for you that the seeds of meaningful work need to be planted. Meaningful work does not just occur, but it needs to be nurtured. Without the proper fuel, individuals and teams cannot be more brilliant."

The team knew what to do and placed the piece of cardboard on their clip. On the back was printed their next leadership lesson.

Leadership Lesson for Teams

How do you make sure that creating meaningful work is a top priority for you as a leader? Having people show up ready to work, enjoying their job, and being ready to eliminate negative ripples builds a stronger and more brilliant team. There are some important activities that you can do as a team to encourage this behavior:

1. *Write a passion statement at the individual level and at a team level. This is more than a mission or vision statement. It is something that fuels us to tackle the day and create positive ripples.*
2. *What is the team excited and passionate about? What are their passion projects that will help the team shine? Capture these!*
3. *Aside from their strengths, what is this team good at? What competencies and skills make this team shine bright? Write these down and share them.*

It was about 10:30 am. Mike informed the group that there would be one last experience on the retreat before they would break for lunch and have some free time.

As they walked back to the main trail, the team was talking about the first three experiences. They were overheard discussing how these exercises would be great for an upcoming leadership meeting. This was the pollination that Jack had envisioned: taking a team on an experience and having them replicate it more broadly across their organization. This pointed to the essence of how teams can shine more brilliant though creating positive ripples and influencing culture.

Leadership Experience #4: Platinum Rule

As the group walked from the butterfly garden together, Mike reached into his burlap bag and held up another stone. "Team Wolfpack, please find the starburst jasper in your bag. Hold it in your hand as we walk to the barn.

This stone is used to improve insight and to clarify what your best self looks like and to appreciate how your best self differs from others' best self. Starburst jasper allows fluidity through the body, removing blockages and increasing the mind and body connection. Sometimes we need to unlearn before we can effectively learn, which can be quite hard for adults."

The team arrived at a small paddock area with a barn. There were two horses out in the paddock standing at the railing and peering over at the group.

Mike said, "Don't worry. They don't bite."

The group began petting the horses' noses.

"This is one of the most special activities on the vineyard. I think groups are going to love this one, so let me know your feedback on it," Mike said. "This horse with the white nose is Cordelia, and the black one over there is named Rosie."

Mike continued, "During this experience we are going to focus on something important that leaders need to prioritize to ensure all the elements of building a brighter team exist, and that is trust. Sometimes people fail to realize that trust is built by encouraging the four 'C's of trust:

- Competence
- Consistency
- Commitment
- Care/Communication"

Mike elaborated, "During this activity we are going to try and build trust with Cordelia and Rosie. I want you to divide up into two teams and follow me into the paddock. One important rule to know is that horses can sense fear, so be calm and relaxed. But these horses are gentle, so don't let that scare you."

"The first element of trust is competence, so I want us to learn how to put the halter on the horse so we can attach a lead."

Mike demonstrated putting the halter on the horse with ease. He asked the teams to put the halter on their horse, with each team member taking turns putting it on and taking it off. This exercise took a bit of effort because some people struggled with getting the horse to comply with them, but ultimately everyone learned (and unlearned in some cases) and successfully put the halter on.

Next, Mike demonstrated how to connect the lead. He touched the horse's neck and gave it a pat, then he clicked his mouth and the horse followed beside him as they walked together in a circle. Mike handed the lead to each team and asked them to attach it to the halter. The team had a task: take turns walking the horse in a circle and then to the other side of the paddock.

The exercise proved interesting. The team could not get the horse to move even with all the clicking and pulling of the lead. They looked at Mike as if to ask him what they were doing wrong.

Mike walked over, grabbed the horse gently by the nose, rubbed it, patted his neck, and then clicked.

Mike said, "There is some unlearning that needs to occur here. Sometimes we prioritize the wrong things, as a team, and forget about what others need. To build trust we must unlearn bad habits that may hinder our progression. The horse requires consistency and care. Everyone needs to demonstrate this on the team. One person cannot care more or more frequently. For the horse to trust us, much like teams we need to consistently show that we care for one another. Now take a moment and show up for the horse in a caring way, and you will all see the difference."

Both teams took the advice and petted the horse, with the first person taking the lead, then the next person, and so on. Everyone had a chance to lead the horses. They all demonstrated consistency. It was a beautiful sight to behold.

When the team brought the horses back, they unhooked the leads, and the horses grabbed a drink from a nearby bucket.

Mike asked the group, "So what did you learn about building trust with horses?"

Lillian opened the conversation. "When you first show care as an individual, the horse is more willing to participate and understands that you are not going to hurt them, and they can trust you."

Kelly chimed in. "Yes, but as a team we all had to do it to ensure the horse trusted all of us. Even though one person on the team gained trust, the horse's progress would have stopped if we hadn't all consistently demonstrated the care."

Mike clapped his hands. "Yes! This is what building more brilliant teams is all about, ensuring trust is built among all members of the team. There is one more piece of building trust, and that is showing that we care through communication, which comes in the form of both verbal and nonverbal communication. We're all going to work with Cordelia. I'll hand Rosie's team a piece of paper with an activity. They can only communicate using nonverbal communication and Cordelia's team has to complete the task."

Mike handed Rosie's team a piece of paper, which laid out these steps:

1. Halter Cordelia.
2. Place a lead on Cordelia.
3. Walk Cordelia in a circle.
4. Walk Cordelia over to the fence.
5. Put a blanket over Cordelia.

Rosie's team was looking around and cupping their mouths. They were strategizing.

The charades and the nonverbal cues they came up with were amazing. All the tasks got completed but not without a little cheating. A few people blurted out words, but the intent of the exercise was to demonstrate the importance of communication in optimizing team performance and building trust.

Mike pulled out another laminated rectangular card. This one was silver and had the next leadership lesson written on it.

Leadership Lesson for Teams

Building trust, while unlearning, is a very important concept. The Golden Rule states that we should treat others as we want to be treated, but fundamentally we should be treating others as they want to be treated. This is the Platinum Rule. Much like the horses, people want to be treated a certain way to establish trust. It's hard to build trust on a team when people assume everyone wants to be treated the same way. How can you as a leader help align your team to be more trusting and more brilliant? Here are some team activities you can do that will encourage trust:

1. *Training and leadership agendas should all have a framework. Start aligning your team meetings in the four "C"s of trust framework to encourage reflection and reinforce the behaviors.*
2. *Set the agenda to train on functional competence and leadership competence.*
3. *Add an agenda item to focus on showing how we care through communication. This can be focused on understanding the organizational priorities and strategy and how we are communicating this strategy consistently.*
4. *The final agenda item for your meeting could be aligned to commitment. This commitment should be to helping one another leverage strengths and how we are unlearning as a team and demonstrating the Platinum Rule.*

"I think people are going to lose trust in me if I don't start feeding you," Mike said to the team. "How about heading to lunch?"

Everyone nodded and followed Mike to a nice area with some shade that overlooked the vineyard's rows of grapevines. One table was elegantly set with a white tablecloth and decked out with grapevines, charcuterie, and sandwiches. The highlight was some honeycomb from the hives in the butterfly garden. The group grabbed some food and sat at the nearby tables.

As they started to eat, they were greeted by another friendly voice. It was Jack!

"Hi, Team Wolfpack!" he said. "A little bee told me that you guys are the Wolfpack. That's a great name. I want to share a story about wolves I think you might enjoy. The Stars and Stones retreat was inspired by a recent hiking trip I took, a trip that fundamentally changed my life. I realized that, prior to my experiences on the trip, I unknowingly operated as a lone wolf. Anyone here prefer to do things on your own or sometimes fail to ask for help with things?"

A couple of hands went up.

"On one of my hikes, I met this woman, Emme, who shared a story with me about a college professor who helped her find her pack. If I recall correctly, Emme's class was learning about what an organization's mission means, and she was asked to think about her personal purpose. Emme struggled with looking within and decided to visit her professor during office hours."

Jack continued, "One day, her professor gave her a little satin bag with a moonstone and a personalized note, which read, 'Sometimes in the dark we need the light of the moon to illuminate the path forward. Different people in your life will serve as your moon if you allow them.' While it took Emme a while to focus time and energy on building her pack, she inspired me to do the same. So, as you proudly named your team Wolfpack, think about the significance and, even more, the opportunity to be the moon for the person to your right and to your left on dark days. We need each other."

Leadership Experience #5: Always Be Proximal

After lunch, Jack walked the team a short distance over to the center of the vineyard, which was where they had originally started. Jack pulled a stone out of his burlap bag and held it up, walking around the circle for all to see.

"Please find your moonstone, hold it in your hand, and close your eyes. Interestingly, moonstone is also called wolf's eye, which this pack may want to call it. This stone promotes inner peace, which leads to emotional healing and spiritual connection. Moonstone centers you, clears scattered thoughts, and calms and relaxes the mind and body. It enables you to live according to your divine purpose. To live your purpose and help others live their purpose, you must keep learning and growth at the heart of what you do. Do you know where we are standing right now?"

The team started opening their eyes.

"This is where us vintners focus on placing ourselves at the center of growth for the vineyard. I want you all to taste some of the different varieties of wine we make here at Stars and Stones."

The group sat at a long table and had their first small tasting glass of wine. The wine was a Chardonnay.

Jack told the team, "The reason I'm sharing this with you is not so much for the wine itself but for you to understand a little about the process of making wine because it's not so dissimilar to team building. Let me explain. I purchased this area in Yountville because it is a blue zone. Blue zones are places where well-being, health, mind, body, and soul are prioritized. Like the moonstone, you are in the right environment to focus on your well-being, which is no different from what you need to build a more brilliant team. Ensuring the environment is right and safe for everyone to grow is ensuring we are focused on wellness."

Half the group sipped the wine, and the other half had some water. The people who had tasted the wine said it was good.

"What is this one called?" Kelly asked.

"Moonstone," Jack smiled. "The lesson here, though, is not how good the wine tastes, but the process to make something brilliant. Do you see those vines over there? They need constant water, pruning, and attention to produce the best output. This is why teams need to place themselves at the center of growth for one another, because we all need constant pruning and refining and nurturing, just like these vines."

The Wolfpack nodded in agreement.

Jack brought out another batch of wine for the group.

"Have a taste of this one," he said. "All wines need different time to grow and develop, just like teams. You may have people on the team who need a little more time, while others may pick things up faster. Wine is the same way. Sometimes waiting produces something very good, and if we rush the process, we could miss key aspects of growth and development. This is the vintner's role, just like everyone on the team's role. Timing is everything when investing in building a brighter team."

When the group finished their tasting, Jack led them to a small shed. He said, "I understand you just went through trust training, so I hope you trust me." He pointed to a large tub filled with grapes. "This is part of the process of wine making!"

The group looked at each other uncomfortably.

"Come on, Wolfpack, get out of your comfort zone, and do the things that you may not think will be fun. Any takers? We need some grape squashers. Take those shoes off and hike up those pants. Let's go, Wolfpack!"

They all removed their shoes and entered the tub as a team. They walked all over the grapes. Everything was awkward and squishy, and they couldn't stop laughing. As they were doing that activity, Jack illuminated why trusting the process was so important when it comes to building brilliant teams.

"Both learning and unlearning will need to occur on the team. People will need to choose the hard things to do. When we pull together as a team and we follow our compass, we can really be brilliant. It won't happen overnight, but it is a process of constant refinement. This team needs to place themselves at the center of each other's growth and closest to the heart. This is what it means to be proximal."

The team stepped out of the tub and cleaned up. They had a great time.

Jack handed them each a rectangular wine label. The Stars and Stones Moonstone wine label appeared on one side, and their next leadership lesson on the other.

Leadership Lesson for Teams

The vintner places themself at the center of the vineyard's growth and follows a process to optimize the output. Teams who want to be brilliant can follow a similar model to ensure constant refinement and growth of one other. As leaders, ask yourselves how you are following the process of wine making on your team.

1. *Start by creating the right environment for learning and growth for your team.*
2. *Water and prune your personal vines at the individual level, which encourages growth and rebirth. Cut away the dead branches and leaves to ensure fresh ideas and perspectives are being shared.*

3. *The timing of when you harvest is no different than deploying your teams' mindsets and strengths at the right time to optimize output.*

4. *Have a process for how your team can develop at the individual, group, and organizational level. If you have the right process, then trusting in the process will bear fruit. Define a growth and development process for your team and hold each other accountable.*

Lillian observed that she never would have thought of these parallels, but that they really made sense. The team agreed and hooked the card onto their bags.

"Okay, are you all ready for the next adventure to challenge you physically and mentally?" Jack asked.

The team seemed eager to learn.

"We have a little bit of a walk over to that hill with the rock face. Let's go!"

Leadership Experience #6: Solutions-Focused Lens

As they walked, Jack engaged the team. "Raise your hand if you strive to achieve very difficult goals."

Everyone raised their hand and looked around.

"In your bags, you will find this bumblebee jasper," he said as he held up a unique yellow and black stone for everyone to see. "This stone helps us to examine opportunities that exist for us to maintain a positive attitude during a time when the journey may be frustrating. The goal of the bumblebee jasper is to help us to see the silver linings while demonstrating a growth mindset. It is said to give you courage to believe in your ability, to see the realities of a current situation, and to appreciate the learning opportunities in finding the way forward."

Jack continued, "There are five 'A's that I want you to remember when you think about choosing a solutions-focused lens. When I learned the message about the bumblebee jasper, I realized that there are some foundational lessons for individuals and for teams to bring these to life in a meaningful way. Each 'A' comes from the inspiration of the stone, which truly illuminates how teams can effectively navigate challenges together. Teams must encourage the use of each person's ability, show up with a positive attitude, appreciate all the learning opportunities, practice accountability, and, as strange as this sounds, encourage anxiety, but in a healthy way. When people are anxious, they feel challenged. And when people are challenged, they can grow faster personally and professionally as they lean into learning the skills needed to meet the challenge. These 'A's illuminate a solutions-focused lens for your team:

- Ability
- Attitude
- Appreciation
- Accountability
- Anxiety"

They all approached the base of the hill where there was a short climb up to a rock face. They could see that on the rock face was a narrow ledge with a rope and a small chasm that needed to be traversed.

"Wolfpack, I am going to lead you up to the rock face and we're going to take a walk across that ledge. The ledge is narrow, but flat. There is a small area that you will need to cross where there is a gap in the rocks. You will need to take a careful step over this gap, but I want you to ensure you're holding onto the rope. Now I'm going to let you all talk this through, but you have 15-minutes, as a team, to traverse the rock face to make the 30-yard walk across. I will be on the other side waiting for you. Wait until I get to the other side before crossing as a team."

The team watched as Jack modeled the way. He faced the wall and stepped side to side slowly. When he reached the small gap in the mountain, he took a large step but held onto the rope. It was not as bad as it looked from down below. He reached the other side and motioned for the team to come across. They started their walk.

Kelly went first. He walked about five yards and stopped. He looked up at the rock wall and saw a message painted on the wall:

Choose your lens and **appreciate** *all the opportunities for learning and growth.*

Kelly pointed out to the rest of the team that there was a saying on the wall, so they wouldn't miss it. The remainder of the team started walking.

After another few big steps Kelly stopped again. The rest of the team was just getting to the first quote when Kelly saw another one painted on the wall.

Building a culture where teams encourage ongoing learning to fuel our ability encourages growth!

Kelly again pointed out the message to the team.

The pace of the team sped up on the mountain, and they almost forgot they were on a narrow ledge. They were eager to see the next quote and read it.

When Kelly reached the next quote, it was near the gap in the mountain. The quote started on one side and ended on the other side, requiring the observer to hold on carefully and read as they crossed:

*When teams lean in to challenges and embrace skill building in the process, this encourages a healthy form of **anxiety** that encourages the way forward.*

When Kelly crossed the gap, he shouted to the team, "Be careful. There's a quote here that spans the gap."

The team was working together brilliantly to cross the rock wall.

Kelly continued as the team followed. He was looking for another quote. In the very last few yards, words began to appear:

*To unleash the brilliance of building brighter teams, choosing your **attitude** while being solutions focused is a culture contagion.*

Jack was waiting on a more open part of the mountain as the team all began to finish. "What did you think of the wall?" he asked them.

"Surprising," Kelly said. "I was not expecting to see the quotes, but they all tied back to your message about the bumblebee jasper. It made the walk more meaningful and exciting. Less stressful."

"I agree," Cole said. "They were so inspiring."

The team was all agreeing.

"Where was the accountability quote?" Giules asked. "I thought there were five 'A's."

Jack pointed up and to his right. Higher up on the rock wall where everyone was standing was a quote in much bigger letters:

*The brightest teams hold focus on **accountability** at the most basic level. This starts with you!*

He took out a rectangular card for each person. It showed a telescope on one side and the next leadership lesson on the other.

Leadership Lesson for Teams

Solutions-focused cultures concentrate on finding ways to navigate challenges together. This means deploying strengths, leveraging team mindsets, trusting one another, and ensuring the environment is set up for team success. As a leadership team, choose your solutions-focused lens by employing the five "A"s as a framework to help your people be more solutions focused:

1. ***Appreciation:*** *Appreciate all the opportunities for [un] learning and growth.*
2. ***Attitude:*** *Choose your attitude. No matter how much knowledge and skill the team has, if the attitude is negative, performance and culture suffer.*
3. ***Anxiety:*** *Meet challenges with learning opportunities to channel anxiety in healthy ways. Find ways to promote growth and development and get people out of their comfort zone.*
4. ***Ability:*** *Create a learning environment that fuels the ability to find new ways of doing things and new solutions.*
5. ***Accountability:*** *What measures do you have in place for personal and professional accountability so the team can be brilliant?*

"OKay, Wolfpack, the sun is starting to set. We are going to head down to the center of the vineyard. You may want to grab a sweater or jacket because the final activity will be after the sun sets."

The team made their way down to the center of the vineyard.

Leadership Experience #7: Shine Brighter and Stronger Together

As the team approached the core of learning and growth, they saw chairs set up around a small fire pit. The sun had already set, and the temperature was dropping. To enhance the environment and keep things cozy, Mike was there with some blankets and hot drinks, and of course some mulled wine for those who wanted to partake. In the center of the rope circle were two telescopes pointing westward. Some of the stars were already shining in the sky and the half-moon was starting to become brighter and more visible.

"Good to see everyone again," Mike said. "I hope your afternoon was fulfilling and inspirational! Have a seat for a minute and relax after that rock wall experience."

The team sat down a for a well-deserved rest. Jack walked up and greeted everyone. He was carrying some Sharpies and a small bag, which he put down on a table behind the fire pit.

"Good evening, everyone. I cannot believe this retreat has to end, but if it must end somewhere it needs to be here at the core of learning and growth."

He passed out a Sharpie and an index card to everyone.

"During the day you have been curating a guide, a compass if you will, to help chart your course to unleash the brilliance of building a brighter team. Before we get into the last experience, I want to do some reflection. Take your Sharpie and put the first letter of the learning that happened at each experience in the upper right-hand corner."

He walked around to each person as they were adding the letters COMPAS. . . .

"Oh," he heard Giules laugh. "These are going to spell 'COMPASS.' What's the last 'S' stand for?"

"That's what we're here for. This retreat is designed to unlock the brilliance of teams, but also to share the importance of building your own personal star system. This retreat would not exist if I hadn't learned about the importance of having a star system in your life. Your star system is made up of individuals who can help you see things differently, clearer, and challenge you, help you grow, and provide the nourishment at the mind, body, and soul. The same trip I was on where I learned about moonstone, I also learned that I was a lone wolf and needed a star system to help me."

He walked over to Uncle Mike and put his hand on his shoulder. "Mike was the first member of my star system. He really has been here for me and has helped me bring this vision to life. Does anyone here have people in their life who could be in their star system?"

Hands went up.

"Well, I encourage you to let those people know how important they are to you, because they may not know, and ask them to be in your star system."

"So, is the last 'S' how to build your star system?" Brad asked.

"Good guess," Jack said, "but no. It's shine! It's shine brighter and stronger together. That is why tonight we are all going to be Stargazers. I learned from someone in my star system that you don't have to be an astrophysicist to appreciate the brilliance of the stars. I have both telescopes set up pointing in the direction of some stars. One is pointing to Betelgeuse, and the other Polaris. I want all of you to come over here and take a look."

They all looked through the telescopes. They seemed unimpressed and unphased by what they saw.

"It was kind of just a blurry dot," Maggie said.

The rest agreed.

"That's right," Jack said. "The average person with a decent telescope only sees a blurry dot when they look at even the brightest stars in our sky. So, why is it important for us to learn what it means to be a Stargazer? It's because Stargazers find the brightness not only in one star but in how the stars are interconnected to shine more brightly together and tell a stronger story together."

Jack pointed with his finger toward Betelgeuse. "I want you all to look into the night sky here. The star you were looking at is called Betelgeuse. Do you know why that star is important? Because it illuminates something much bigger. Does anyone know which constellation Betelgeuse is in?"

Kelly spoke up. "It's the shoulder of Orion."

"Yes!" Jack said.

Jack pointed out each star in Orion and confirmed with the team that they could visualize the constellation.

"The star looks better without the telescope," Giules laughed, "and I see the whole constellation."

"How about the other star, Polaris, which is more familiarly known as the North Star. Who knows what constellation it's in?" Jack asked.

It was quiet.

"Polaris is in the Little Dipper, or Ursa Minor."

Jack pointed out the Big Dipper and the Little Dipper. Heads nodded.

"As we think about unleashing our team's brilliance, we sometimes need to take a step back and look at the whole picture. There will always be a couple of bright stars in an organization, but if we truly want to unleash the brilliance of a brighter team, then we need teams to illuminate what happens when we're connected. When entire teams are brilliant, anything they touch lights up, and they illuminate the people around them and make them stronger. Teams are exactly like constellations. Individuals, individual mindsets, and strengths are essential to a high-performing team, but when combined with other strengths, they exponentially unleash more power. To be a Stargazer is to ensure the team is focused on a 'we' mindset versus a 'me' mindset."

The glow of the fire lit up Jack's face as he continued passionately. "So if you want to take your team to the next level, seek to create an environment to collaborate better, trust better, and enjoy work more. It's up to you! You need to be a Stargazer and help your team shine more brightly and stronger together. The more Stargazers you have, the faster you can unleash the brilliance within your team."

Jack reached in his bag and handed each person on the team a rectangular card. On the front, each card featured the word "Stargazer" and a different constellation of stars that ran through the "a" in the word, but they all shared the same final leadership lesson on the back.

Leadership Lesson for Teams

1. *Let the COMPASS framework be your team's guide.*
2. *Be a Stargazer!*

"Jack, why is the 'a' yellow in 'Stargazer' on the back of this card?" Brad asked.

"Can anyone tell me?" Jack responded.

Giules spoke up again. She had been quiet most of the day, but the energy at night was getting her more involved. "You mentioned earlier that brighter teams focus on illuminating everything around them and everything they touch. Just like the touch of the constellation illuminated the 'a' in Stargazer, the energy of your star system makes you shine bright!"

"That's exactly right! The people in my star system helped illuminate me, and they inspired me to create the 'Stars and Stones' experience and help build brighter teams. I want to give you something to put in your bag that will remind you to shine more brightly!"

Jack dug into his bag, looking for the next thing. He glanced up to see Grayce standing next to Mike. "Grayce! What are you doing here?" He walked over for a hug.

"I didn't want to miss your first corporate retreat! Go ahead," she said.

"Happy to have another person in my star system here, Team Wolfpack. That's Grayce, and she was the person in my star system who taught me how to be a Stargazer."

Jack reached into the bag and took out a small wooden star for each team member. "I want you to take this this star and put it into your bag filled with all the reminders and lessons you need to guide your team to shine more brightly. There is enough room on here to write your team's Be mindset in the middle so you can all remember to do what?" he asked, holding his hand up to his ear to listen for their response.

"Be Bold!" they collectively called out.

"Well, shine brightly everyone, *be inspired, and remember that you're brilliant!*"

Jack turned to Grayce. "Do you want to add any closing comments for the team?"

She shook her head no and said, "That was brilliant, Jack."

He smiled. "Actually, speaking of brilliant, that reminds me. As this retreat comes to an end, it's just the beginning of your journey, Team Wolfpack. But there are some other individuals who may not be here with us right now, who have also been focused on being brilliant."

Jack looked to the dark sky illuminated with stars and said, "So tell me, Stargazers, what will your Be Brilliant journal say and how will you unleash the brilliance of building brighter teams?"

Connect with us at www.leadershipfables.com

leadership fables

Acknowledgments

Thank you to the greatest pollinator I know, who has inspired this journey to the stars! I am grateful to those in my life who help me grow personally and professionally. To my mom, dad, and sister, thanks for your ongoing love and support. To my wife and three daughters, thank you for encouraging me to dream big. And a special thank-you to everyone in my star system who has helped illuminate the ways I can shine more brightly. We are brighter together!

Love always, Michael

My heart is smiling as I author this important piece of our story. I am eternally grateful for this gift. It is the people in my life who are the heart of ongoing learning and growth. All my love and expressions of gratitude are extended to my mom, dad, and sister for sharing roots to grow; to my husband and two daughters for encouraging my wings to fly; and to each additional member of my star system for inspiring the ebb and flow of our journey. We are certainly brighter, better, richer, and stronger, **together**.

Love and gratitude always, Katie xo

About the Authors

Michael G. Frino has over 25 years of professional experience working for Fortune 500 companies in sales, leadership, and organizational development across the payroll/human resources, pharmaceutical, and med-tech industries. Michael finds his flow state today from helping organizations transform their culture with a focus on the growth and development of human beings. His curiosity on how organizations optimize performance at work inspired him to obtain his PhD in organizational learning and leadership in 2010 and to embrace opportunities to help individuals, groups, and organizations reach their peak potential. He co-wrote the *Wall Street Journal* bestselling book *The Beekeeper: Pollinating Your Organization for Transformative Growth* and has published multiple papers on how to optimize human performance with his research and growth partner, Katie P. Desiderio.

Katie P. Desiderio counts her blessings starting with the people in her life, which guides her approach to work where her focus is on every organization's most important asset – you! Her personality and behavioral attributes emphasize collaboration and all things that keep human beings in focus, which fuels her intrapreneurial spirit. As an athlete, she found flow in sport and later discovered flow at work to fuel her professional trajectory. After working for several years in corporate marketing, Katie chose a second career in higher education, where she celebrates the honor of being the first female chairperson of the Economics and Business Department at the sixth-oldest institution in America and the first to educate women. As the mama of two extraordinary girls, she is committed to the development of rising leaders, namely in the spirit of leading from any seat. Along with her work as a tenured professor of management at Moravian University, Desiderio is Principal Partner in Learning of Proximal Development, LLC, an Authorized DiSC Partner, specializing in leadership development and the advancement of performance through learning. Katie's personal mission is grounded in her r^2C model where she has devoted her work to *recognize* what we give our time and energy to grows, to *reflect* on how we [choose to] interact with and see the world, and, at the heart of her approach, to *connect* with why this fuels transformative growth. This model is delicately nurtured in the interplay of our mindset and our [mindful] behaviors, so when she falls along the way, she chooses to fall up. This inspires her to lead with *grace* while tickling curiosity and encouraging discovery in working with and through others. As a scholar-practitioner, she has been co-authoring journal articles, conference proceedings, and now this book with her growth partner. Join them on this journey to inspire how you will pollinate the world!

Index

Page number followed by *f* refers to figure.

Abilities:
  encouraging, 163, 166
  relying on, 69–70
  working within confines of, 61–64
Accountability, 163, 165, 166
Always Be Proximal, 135–136, 158–162
Antares, 44
Anxiety, 163, 165, 166
Appreciation, 163, 164, 166
Attitude, 55, 56, 162, 163, 165, 166
Authentic conversation, 147

Be Brilliant, 172. *See also* Brilliance
Bees and beehives, 72, 144
Beehive Cluster, 71, 73, 93
Being true to who you are, 41–43
Be mindsets, ix–x, 13, 133, 143–146
Be Proximal, 13, 108, 133, 135–136, 158–162
Best self:
  clarifying, 28, 29, 153
  concentrating on being, 55, 56, 68
    (*See also* Transformation)
Betelgeuse, 169
Big Dipper, 30–31, 169
Bravery, 74
Brilliance, 20, 21, 148–149, 160–162, 170
Bumblebee jasper, 55, 56, 67–69, 74, 121, 162, 163

Butterfly, 43–44, 46, 150
Butterfly effect, 45, 134
Butterfly jasper, 38, 41, 43, 121, 149
Butterfly Nebula, 44, 134

Cairn, 84–85
Cancer sign/constellation, 70–72, 74, 80
Care, in trust building, 107, 110, 135, 153–157
Castor, 71
Centered, being, 21
Challenging situations, 44–45, 61–64, 114
Changes, 53–55, 103
Chaos theory, 134
Chess, 32, 40
  at corporate retreats, 133–134, 146–148
  with Geo, 61–64, 106, 107, 126–127
Choice:
  of attitude, 165, 166
  of lens, 21, 28–29, 92, 142
  of mindset, 133, 143–146
  of who and how you want to be, 103
Choose Your Be Mindset, 133, 143–146
Clarity, 28, 29, 93, 153

Classical music, 77
Commitment, in trust building, 107, 110, 135, 153, 157
Communication, in trust building, 153, 155–157
COMPASS framework, 133–140, 140*f*
   Always Be Proximal, 135–136
   Choose Your Be Mindsets, 133
   as guide in leading teams, 142
      (*See also* Leadership guide)
   Meaningful Work, 134
   Open Eyes, Mind, Ears, and Heart, 133–134
   Platinum Rule, 134–135
   Shine Brighter and Stronger Together, 136
   Solutions-Focused Lens, 136
Competence, in trust building, 107, 110, 135, 153, 154, 157
Conflict, 31, 93
Connections, 37, 46
   to being a lone wolf, 86
   making, 106–107 (*See also* Star systems)
   meaningful, 91–97
   meetings vs., 107–108
   and self-reliance, 73
   spiritual, 81
   to stars, 67–73
   that change a life, 103
Consistency, in trust building, 107, 110, 135, 153–155
Core of learning and growth:
   at campground, 13, 18–19, 21, 26–27
   for corporate retreats, 133, 159
   creating a, 124
   placing yourself at center of, 135
   pollinating others in, 72
   as proximal, 92
   star system help in keeping at, 109
Corporate retreats:
   COMPASS framework for, 133–140
   leadership guide for (*see* Leadership guide)
   vision for, 124–125, 127

Costars, 54, 69. *See also* Connections
Courage, 55, 74
Creativity, 70, 93
Culture, 20–21
Curiosity, 102, 136

Direction, 91–93, 139
Disturbances, 25–33. *See also* Ripples
   for growth and development, 31–32
   leaning into, 28–29
   in plans, 25–26, 29–30

Emotions, 41, 43, 70–71, 81
Emotional intelligence, 73
Encouragement, 104
Environment:
   for growth, 31–33
   impact of trivial things on, 45
   for seeing beauty, 101–102
Epistemological crisis, 117

Finer things in life, 20–21
Five "A"s, 163–166
Flow, 114–115, 117, 123, 136
Focus, 85, 123, 127, 136. *See also* Lens(es)
Forgetting, 31–33, 37, 117
Four "C"s to trust building, 107, 110, 135, 153–157
Frustration, 55, 56, 68, 162

Grounding, 41, 46, 81
Growth:
   being partner for, 103
   core of learning and (*see* Core of learning and growth)
   environment for, 31–33
   in nature, 52–53
   opportunities for, 163, 164
   placing yourself at core of, 133
   small changes for, 53–55
   star system as source of, 107–109, 115
   transformation supporting, 46
      (*See also* Transformation)
Growth mindset, 55, 68, 162

Harmony, 19, 21
Horses, 135, 153–156

Impression jasper, 104, 121, 146
Innovation, 102
Interactions, 31, 96, 107–108. *See also*
    Connections
Introspection, 93

Leadership guide, 141–172
    Always Be Proximal, 158–162
    Choose Your Be Mindset, 143–146
    Meaningful Work, 149–152
    Open Eyes, Mind, Ears, and
        Heart, 146–149
    Platinum Rule, 152–158
    Shine Brighter and Stronger
        Together, 167–172
    Solutions-Focused Lens, 162–166
Leadership metaphors:
    for achieving flow, 114
    butterflies as, 150
    butterfly effect as, 45
    Butterfly Nebula as, 134
    Cancer as, 70–71, 93–94
    constellations as, 53, 107–109,
        123, 170–171
    lake ripples as, 28
    landscapes as, 114
    Orion as, 107, 169
    Polaris as, 169
    Scorpio as, 44–45
    Solutions-Focused Lens area as, 136
    starburst galaxies as, 31–32
    Ursa Major as, 30–31
Learner's mind, 21
Learning:
    core of growth and (*see* Core of
        learning and growth)
    epistemological crisis in, 117
    forgetting/unlearning in, 31–33, 37,
        117, 153, 161
    missing moments of, 56
    opportunities for, 163, 164
Lens(es):
    choice of, 21, 28–29, 92, 142
    for seeing beauty, 101–102
    solutions-focused, 85, 136, 162–166

Libra sign, 80
Light pollution, 101
Little things, importance of, 46
Lone wolf(-ves), 69–73
    and appreciation for other
        people, 78–79
    being a, 77–87
    journey of, 93
    and mentors, 77, 80–83
    moving away from mentality
        of, 122
    in nature, 85–86
    and need for a pack, 107
    and personal purpose, 82–83
    preference for, 79–80
    and readiness for star systems,
        105–106
Love, 19

Marriage of Figaro (Mozart), 77
Meaningful Work, 134, 149–152
Meetings, connections vs., 107–108
Mentors, 77, 80–83, 86
Mind–body connection, 30, 33, 37,
    46, 104, 153
Mindset(s), ix–x
    Be, 13, 133, 143–146
    of Be Proximal, 13, 21
    as core of learning and growth,
        13, 18–19, 21
    growth, 55, 68, 162
    of a learner, 21
Moonstone, 79–83, 86, 93,
    121, 158, 159

Nature, 21
    beauty of, 51–52
    costars in, 54, 69
    enjoying, 103
    growth in, 52–53
    link to, 21
    peace in, 79, 84

Open Eyes, Mind, Ears, and Heart,
    133–134, 146–149
Opportunities, 68, 162–164
Orion, 107, 169

Pack:
  building a, 107 (*See also* Star systems)
  having a, 83, 86 (*See also* Lone wolf(-ves))
Pack mentality, 104–105
Passion, 151, 152
Path(s):
  difficult, rewards of, 114
  to move forward, 93
  that balance challenges with skill, 115, 117
  true, discovering your, 93–94
Peace, 77, 79, 81, 84
People. *See also* Connections
  appreciation for, 78–79
  asking deeper, more personal questions about, 81–82
  who support you, 122
Performance improvement, 115, 135
Perseverance, 61–64
Platinum Rule, 134–135, 152–158
Polaris (North Star), 169
Pollinators, 44, 72, 94
Pollux, 71
Positive attitude, 55, 56, 68, 74, 162, 163
Presence of the mind, 81
Priorities, 153, 154
Purpose:
  clarifying, 29
  company, 82–83
  divine, living according to, 81
  personal, 82–83, 107, 158
  shared, 115

Recency bias effect, 55, 104
Regulus, 71
Relationships. *See also* Connections
  emotionally strong, 20
  grounded in trust, 117
  love and harmony in, 19
  for personal growth and development, 31 (*See also* Star systems)
Resilience, 74, 93
Retreats, *see* Corporate retreats
Ripples and ripple effect, 28

butterfly effect with, 151
in life, impact of, 30
of little things, 32, 46
with negative consequences, 151
positive and negative, 134
Risky situations, 44–45

Scorpio constellation, 44
Scorpions, 40, 42–44
Scorpio sign, 80
Self-confidence, 55, 68
Self-discovery, 93
Self-reliance, 69–73, 86. *See also* Lone wolf(-ves)
Shine Brighter and Stronger Together, 136, 167–172
Sierra Nevadas, 52–54
Solution focus, 85
Solutions-Focused Lens, 136, 162–166
Soul searching, 107
Starburst galaxies, 31–33
Starburst jasper, 28, 30, 33, 121, 152–153
Star clusters, 71–73
Stargazers, 94, 96, 168–170. *See also* Connections
Star systems, x, 94–96, 105–110
  building your, 122–129
  cohesive teams formed by, 109, 136
  in helping achieve and sustain flow, 114–115, 117
  insights from, 139
  shining brighter with, 136, 167–172
  as source of growth, 107–109, 116
Strategic thinking, 134
Strategy, 146, 147
Stress, 28, 32, 136

Teams:
  achieving and sustaining flow in, 117
  COMPASS framework for, 133–140 (*See also* Leadership guide)
  formed by star systems, 109, 136 (*See also* Star systems)
  optimizing performance of, 135

Teamwork, 134, 146
Telescope tree, 39, 40
Togetherness, 51–57. *See also*
    Star systems
Tranquility, 104
Transformation, 37–47, 150
    of butterflies, 43–44
    through challenging or risky
        situations, 44–45
    through the unexpected, 37–40
True path, discovering your, 93–94
Trust:
    building, 107, 110, 134–135, 153–157
    identifying people you can, 107
    in the process, 160–161
    relationships grounded in, 117
    on teams, 115

Truth, personal, 93
Tunnel tree, 39

Unlearning, 31–33, 37, 117, 153, 161
Ursa Major, 31
Ursa Minor, 169

Venus, 19–21
Vineyard, 17–18, 20, 68–69, 122–125,
    127–129, 133–140. *See also*
    Corporate retreats
Vulnerability, 69, 105, 147

Wishing, 40
Wonder, sense of, 136
Work, meaningful, 134, 149–152

Katie and Michael are *Wall Street Journal* bestselling authors of *The Beekeeper: Pollinating your Organization for Transformative Growth.*

Learn The Art of Being Proximal

Transform Yourself!

Transform Teams!

Transform Culture!

Become a Pollinator!

Become a **Be Keeper!**

Quotes

"Weaving storytelling and science, Desiderio and Frino provide leaders from all walks of life with sound advice for generating growth–personal. organizational, and societal. This is a wonderful read that can transform your life and your environment!"

Dr. Tal Ben-Shahar
Author | Speaker
Taught Harvard University's most popular course

"In the tradition of the blockbuster book *Who Moved My Cheese?* (1998) by Spencer Johnson, corporate veterans Desiderio and Frino have crafted a business fable that metaphorically compares beekeeping with leading a business. Creatively written, cleverly packaged advice for organizational leaders. As business fables go, this one largely succeeds."

KIRKUS
Book Reviews

WWW.leadershipfables.com